THE FOOD OF

OAXACA

THE FOOD OF
OAXACA

Recipes and Stories from Mexico's Culinary Capital

Alejandro Ruiz

WITH CARLA ALTESOR

With a Foreword by Enrique Olvera

Photographs by Nuria Lagarde

ALFRED A. KNOPF   NEW YORK   2020

THIS IS A BORZOI BOOK PUBLISHED BY ALFRED A. KNOPF

English translation copyright © 2020 Alfred A. Knopf,
a division of Penguin Random House LLC
Photographs © 2020 by Nuria Lagarde

All rights reserved. Published in the United States by Alfred A. Knopf,
a division of Penguin Random House LLC, New York, and distributed in Canada
by Penguin Random House Canada Limited, Toronto. Originally published in
Mexico in slightly different form by Sicomoro Ediciones, Mexico City, in 2018.
Copyright © 2018 by Sicomoro Ediciones.

www.aaknopf.com

Knopf, Borzoi Books, and the colophon are registered
trademarks of Penguin Random House LLC.

Library of Congress Cataloging-in-Publication Data
Names: Ruiz, Alejandro, author.
Title: The food of Oaxaca : recipes and stories from Mexico's culinary capital / Alejandro Ruiz.
Description: First edition. | New York : Alfred A. Knopf, 2020. | Includes index. |
Identifiers: LCCN 2019049861 (print) | LCCN 2019049862 (ebook) |
ISBN 9780525657309 (hardback) | ISBN 9780525657316 (ebook)
Subjects: LCSH: Cooking, Mexican. | Cooking—Mexico—Oaxaca. | LCGFT: Cookbooks.
Classification: LCC TX716.M4 R847 2020 (print) | LCC TX716.M4 (ebook) |
DDC 641.5972/74—dc23
LC record available at https://lccn.loc.gov/2019049861
LC ebook record available at https://lccn.loc.gov/2019049862

Jacket design by Kelly Blair

Manufactured in China
First American Edition

To the memory of
VICENTA OLMEDO

To my wife and children
LILIANA, MAGALY, ALEJANDRO, ISABELLA, AND PAOLO

To my siblings
MARCO, NORMA, JESÚS, AND LOURDES

CONTENTS

FOREWORD

by Enrique Olvera

Travel nourishes us in the most unexpected of ways; when we set out on a journey, there is always the risk—or the hope—that we'll be transformed by the places and people who cross our path. Sometimes these encounters become great anecdotes, others not so much. We travel from one point to another, and into our own inner selves.

My journeys to the interior of Oaxaca state were a doorway that I crossed through into a universe different from my own, yet at the same time full of familiar sensations, aromas, and flavors. Oaxacan cuisine is as vast as the state's territories: the valley, the different mountain ranges, the isthmus, and the coast. One can lose oneself in its richness, however, I had the fortune to discover Oaxaca with Chef Alejandro Ruiz. I call it that—fortune—because Alejandro holds the keys to Oaxaca, and as a good Oaxacan citizen he has always been generous with his time and knowledge about the food of his birthplace.

A few years ago Alejandro and I took a trip to the Oaxacan coast. The journey was long, so we had to stop to eat at some point, and there, in the middle of the mountains' depths, I discovered the taste of chicatana ants—one of the most delicious things I've tried in my life. These ants emerge only once a year, after the first rain, and they are gathered to be cooked parsimoniously in salsas that have become emblematic of certain regions of Oaxaca.

Oaxacan cuisine and its ingredients have always been there, vast and generous, ready to surprise any palate, but also ready to take thousands of different forms. My encounter with the chicatana ants' flavor was translated into one of the most emblematic dishes at my Mexico City restaurant Pujol: the smoking leek, with baby corn with chicatana mayonnaise, that welcomes our diners and situates them in a Mexican context.

In his own way, Alejandro interprets Oaxacan cooking because he knows and respects it deeply, because his dishes show us new facets of this cuisine, yet remain tremendously familiar to us. He fearlessly incorporates his own wanderings through different kitchens in order to show us a daring side of Oaxacan gastronomy, a side that still honors the richness of its past, its earth, and its ingredients. In this book, Alejandro shares the keys to Oaxacan cooking with us and delights us with the bounty of the food from his homeland.

INTRODUCTION

Oaxacan food is one of Mexico's most revered cuisines. Oaxaca is the birthplace of corn, and is home to fifty to sixty different species that are transformed and cooked into a myriad of forms. Made up of eleven regions each featuring distinct cultural and linguistic traits, Oaxaca enjoys some of the most exceptional biodiversity in Mexico, as becomes clear when visiting the main market or Mercado de Abastos, which spans more than thirty acres and offers an infinite array of goods, from produce to food stalls, cookware, and crafts.

This enormous gastronomic wealth has its roots in ancestral ingredients, heavy with spiritual and festive ramifications that seamlessly converge. Oaxaca's dishes, with their foundation of corn, chocolate, chiles, and spices, reflect the marriage of its indigenous roots and technique with the imprint of Spanish influence. The balanced diet that has fed Mexicans for millennia is a core part of our identity, arrived at by collaboration, respect, and responsibility to our land of origin. The preservation of this patrimonial bridge and its link to the future is a major challenge and responsibility, and is vital to the conservation of what many consider the soul of Mexican food.

My siblings and I were born in La Raya de Zimatlán, a rural town of some thirty families in the Zaachila region of the Mexican state of Oaxaca, about twelve miles south of Oaxaca city. La Raya doesn't appear on any maps. People say it was established to buffer disputes between the Zapotecs from Zaachila and the Mixtecs from Zimatlán, the indigenous peoples who often quarreled over two subjects: land and women.

My parents, Vicenta and Joaquín, were from Zaachila and Zimatlán, respectively, and I was their first child. After me came Marco, Norma, Jesús (called Chucho), and Lourdes. We were a farming family. From the time we were small, my brother Marco and I would go to the nearby mountain to tend the milpa.

The milpa is an essential part of my story. The word comes from the Nahuatl milpan, which means "sown parcel on top of." It is a traditional, self-sustaining, carefully balanced agricultural system, where different plants are planted together to boost growth, repel pests, and improve flavor. The most commonly grown crop is corn, which is usually accompanied by beans, squash, peppers, tomatoes, herbs, and many others. It is the Mexican version of the three sisters method of growing, which is otherwise known as the "Mesoamerican triad." Other benefits are the efficient use of space to increase yields, and the diversity this provides, which improves soil health and attracts pollinators and wildlife.

There are many types of milpas, and each is a unique reflection of the characteristics of the soil, the climate, the native species, and the local traditions and expertise, as well as the culinary tastes, or needs, of the farmer. This way of growing remains essential to Mexican cuisine, and is the backbone of our rural food sovereignty.

Growing up, Marco and I would plant tomatoes, harvest beans, and graze livestock at the milpa, but we also had to care for our younger siblings and teach them to work the land themselves. Afternoons were for work, and by nightfall we were tired. We attended the local elementary school and lived close to our grandparents, aunts, and uncles, sheltered by the privilege of belonging to a family. So passed my earliest years.

I was barely twelve years old when my mother died in a tragic accident. It was one night in June, La Noche de San Juan. My mother and father had gone to visit friends, and in a moment of misunderstanding heightened by alcohol, guns were fired and my mother was killed. The loss was devastating for our whole family, and profoundly changed the way we lived. My brother Marco went to live in Mexico City with relatives, and Norma, Lourdes, and Chucho went to live with our grandparents. I stayed in La Raya with our father, who had also lost any semblance of family structure along with the mother of his children. The years that followed were tough in ways that are difficult to imagine. All of us siblings separated, the smallest ones here, the older ones there, and me on my own with very little on which to survive. What I could do was work. I milked the neighbor's cow and ate what I found at the milpa or what my aunts served me. With the dissolution of my family, I felt constantly like I had suddenly stopped being part of something larger than myself. Work was my only tool for survival during those years of mourning and scarcity.

When I was fifteen I left La Raya for the first time to seek work in Oaxaca city. I knocked on many doors that didn't open, but nothing could deter me. I had already survived the unthinkable.

After working for a while at different places in Oaxaca, I decided to move to Puerto Escondido, by the sea, and take a course on food and beverages. I had seen Puerto Escondido only in photos and it looked like a paradise, but my experience there surpassed all of my expectations for growth and freedom.

Puerto Escondido gave me the distance I needed for reconciliation. I lived there for ten years, making peace with my past and making up for lost time alongside my brother Marco, who caught up with me there after two years. We worked, found our callings, and met people from many different walks of life. We learned English and made contacts, and I became a father.

Marco and I returned to Oaxaca city after ten years to reunite with our younger siblings, now grown men and women. Norma and Lourdes were administrators, Jesús had become an attorney. The youngest three decided it was time to support their older brothers, and they went to work so that Marco and I could study. All five of us moved into one house and helped each other get ahead, just as we had been taught as children. Together we recovered the feeling of belonging to a family that we had lost when our mother died.

Back in Oaxaca city, I eventually went to work at Hotel Casa Oaxaca. First, I assisted at the reception desk, but little by little I earned a place in the kitchen. Eventually, I became the hotel's chef, and I used this opportunity to build the platform I needed to follow my calling.

Casa Oaxaca is a seventeenth-century colonial home that was bought and restored as a hotel by a German couple who fell in love with Oaxaca. I practically lived there, helping out as a gardener, receptionist, waiter, housekeeper, plumber, and cook. From the minute I walked in, I knew that this was the place where I wanted to open my restaurant. My siblings also found Casa Oaxaca to be an ideal place to work and establish themselves according to the lessons our mother had imparted to us.

While working at Casa Oaxaca, I traveled to Europe, visiting Germany, Austria, and Spain. I learned everything I could about technique and how to run a kitchen, but by far the greatest lesson was the recognition of my Oaxacan origin, of my palate, trained by a countryside upbringing that guarded ancient and unique flavors. I returned home with an eagerness to share this revelation with the world.

That yearning was satisfied in 2003, as we opened the doors to Casa Oaxaca, the restaurant. I wanted to showcase my personal evolution by incorporating new techniques, and honoring what I'd eaten in Oaxaca all my life, but presenting it in a bold new way, and doing it in a way in which I could be successful, without betraying the place of my birth. The restaurant quickly became an iconic culinary destination. My goal was, and has always been, to provide a platform for Oaxaca's gastronomic wealth, and to extend its branches to its native people. In Oaxaca, when you enter a house, they greet you by saying "Drink a mezcalito" or "Have a little mole," which in reality means, "It's a pleasure to have you in my home." That is what we strive for in our restaurants.

Currently my family, partners, and I oversee both Casa Oaxaca kitchens, plus Casa Oaxaca Café, Oaxacalifornia, which specializes in seafood, Guzina Oaxaca (in Mexico City), and Portozuelo in Zimatlán de Álvarez, a countryside orchard with a rustic open-air kitchen where we cater private events. In the nearly five acres that encompass Portozuelo, we are able to grow 70 percent of the daily produce needed for two of our restaurants. Our idea here is to give life to the earth so that the roots and the wisdom aren't lost. It is in this place that I feel I've come full circle, a refuge where I can show my kids how I grew up and teach them and all who care to visit about the special connections between the land, our heritage, and my food.

HOW TO USE THIS BOOK

This is a book of recipes, but the recipes are not classified in any traditional order. It's irrelevant whether they are starters or main courses, and the same goes for their level of difficulty or the appropriate occasion for serving them. I've arranged these recipes according to a particular context: each chapter contains recipes associated with a specific time and place in my life.

For the most part, these are not simple recipes. They come from the collective imagination of my community, which time has proven, which don't belong to any one person but rather to everyone, thus demanding great respect. In translating them into precise quantities and cooking times, we run the risk of losing something.

The measurements used in each of these recipes are a guide, yet there are many factors to consider: climate, geographic location, the freshness of your ingredients, and so forth.

Take the masa in the recipe for tortillas (page 11). How fresh your corn is, how much water is added, whether your masa has been mixed with masa harina (something that should not be done, but that happens in various tortilla bakeries, known as tortillerías), what season it is, if the weather is hot or humid—all of these things will affect your cooking. Even geography makes a difference. For example, baking at an altitude of 2,500 feet above sea level requires crucial changes in a recipe, such as reducing the amount of baking powder and sugar and raising the amount of liquids and the oven temperature.

The time estimates are also a guide that does not pretend to be exact, as they, too, depend on variable factors. For example, when people who know their way around a kitchen make a dish, it will probably take less time than it would for those who only cook occasionally. If a recipe hasn't been prepared more than five times, or if an unknown technique must be incorporated, that will increase the preparation time. Some people prefer to have all their ingredients, their *mise en place*, ready before starting to cook, while others will go about chopping or doing two steps at a time as they advance. Technical details, such as the heat from a burner or an oven's calibration, are different in each kitchen, and human errors—if the heat was set on high, then the telephone rang and you forgot to turn it down—are things that could cause a sauce to reduce in more or less time than indicated. That is why, apart from time, to get optimal results you should also pay attention to visual, olfactory, and auditory cues.

The salt we used to prepare these recipes is a sea salt from the coasts of Oaxaca. If you can't get sea salt, kosher salt can be used in the same quantities. However, if you use table salt instead, we recommend adding it in smaller proportions and tasting as you go, since a tablespoon of table salt contains more crystals by volume than a tablespoon of sea salt.

In the first chapter, "Origins," you'll find recipes from my childhood. These are the dishes of my family, of my town, and of the state of Oaxaca. Putting them down on paper was a challenge, as codifying these recipes goes against their essence: they come from an oral tradition, not written cookbooks. They were born from the earth, with the rains or with the dry spells, they are the terroir of Oaxaca. I learned to cook these dishes by watching the women in the family cook. Basic questions about preparations, ingredients, or timing were always met with vague answers: "You do it how we've always done it." "Put in as much as it takes." "Cook it for as long as it needs." "Make it what it ought to be." "Make it just as they've done it from the beginning." In these pages, you will see recipes recorded as they are, as they ought to be.

The dishes from the second chapter, "The Coast," are drawn from my time by the ocean. They are the recipes I learned at an age of impatience and fun and their flavors are similarly less complex, more frank, but by no means any less Oaxacan.

The recipes from the third chapter, "Casa Oaxaca," are the cumulative result of the foods of my youth, my travels, and my training. They incorporate multiple sauces, cooking techniques, and decorative condiments, and can take several days to prepare (there are a few salsas that actually benefit from being made in advance). These recipes are the culmination of the chapters that precede them, and you will see in them the evolution of my cooking.

SOME WORDS OF ADVICE

- Read the recipe from start to finish a couple of times before beginning.

- Consult the list of ingredients and make sure you have everything on hand. For example, if the recipe calls for a cup of chopped chiles, chop them and then measure them before you begin.

- Plan your timing: check whether anything should be made the night before, whether any preparation (for example, a reduction) takes a few hours, or whether something needs time to rest. Take into account that preparing more than one recipe at a time will increase the overall time needed.

- Respect the order in which each step is listed. Familiarize yourself with the recipe before making changes, especially if it is your first time cooking it, since substitutions that are not specified can result in complications.

- Guide yourself not only by the time indicated in each step, but also by the sensory cues described.

- Definitions of culinary terms widely used in Oaxaca can be found in the glossary, on page 201.

- Most of the ingredients—including the dried chiles—called for in these recipes can be found in your local grocery store or ordered online. Some ingredients, such as hoja santa or fresh epazote, are available at Mexican grocery stores or markets.

- Several of the recipes in this book such as Masa from La Raya de Zimatlán (page 8) and Pumpkin Candied in Piloncillo (page 62) call for you to use lime, also known as slaked lime, calcium hydroxide, or cal, a highly alkaline substance. Lime is mildly corrosive, so be careful when using it. It can be purchased online.

THE FOOD OF

OAXACA

PART ONE ORIGINS

Where we come from determines who we are, and how we see the world. In my case, my place of origin is Oaxaca, in the broadest sense, but this chapter is really a collection of the recipes from which my cooking emerged.

I come from a rural family from the central valley of Oaxaca. I was raised in the countryside, and my ways of living and cooking are well rooted in the land and its gifts. The milpa—the Mesoamerican technique of planting several crops on a single parcel of land, taking advantage of the special growing characteristics of each one—is the context of my childhood. Ever since I was a child, the milpa has been the landscape of my life, a source of bounty, a place of work, and the provider of ingredients and flavors.

This age-old system of production directly shaped my first years. In rural Mexico, as opposed to in the cities, agricultural cycles and celebrations of both religious and private natures mark the lives of small towns and their inhabitants, and this is particularly true in the fields of Oaxaca. During my childhood I, like the other children in my community, helped my parents to plant and to harvest, spending hours observing how the corn plants grew, how their young ears and kernels formed, how first came blossoms and then squashes. I killed time during those long days in the field tasting local herbs like chepiche, hierba de conejo, and quelites that protect the earth, while grazing the family cow. I gathered chapulines—grasshoppers, a Mexican delicacy—during the rainy season, as well as eggs and beans.

In the Oaxacan countryside, traditionally, men's hands produce and women's hands transform. I brought my mother corn to nixtamalize, or transform into masa. Each day at home we ate Oaxacan tostadas and dry tortillas with some kind of broth, beans, tamales, salsas, and, on good days, freshly made tortillas. These were simple, delicious foods cooked directly over the fire on a traditional clay comal or griddle—everyday flavors without which I would feel lost.

During the rainy season, the whole family gathered to make soup from guías (squash plant runners), and when special occasions arose, the women came together for celebrations, or mayordomías, gatherings that require coordination and knowledge to foster teamwork, unity, harmony, and heritage, passed from generation to generation. These were the best culinary schools I could possibly attend. When the women gathered to cook for days at a time, and the children played and ran errands, I watched and learned the exercise in generosity that is feeding one's loved ones. In those kitchens equipped with only fire, clay, and wood, I learned essential lessons, in a classroom whose language is subtle, in which there is no competition, only cooperation, in which there are no orders, only looks of approval.

The flavors of the field fixed the taste and seasoning of my palate. These ingredients are the foundation of what I cook today at my restaurants. Life in this community defined how I work. It taught me the value of sharing, of generosity, and of working together to bring joy to diners. These are lessons that I continue to draw from today.

THE UNIVERSE IN A TORTILLA

Corn is our blood.
—NAHUA SAYING

Tortillas, memelas, tacos, tlacoyos, tostadas, sopes, dobladas, tetelas, chilaqui-les, empanadas, quesadillas, molotes, garnachas, tamales, enchiladas, pozole, huaraches, tlayudas, champurrados, and atoles flow through every Mexican.

Corn masa is our sustenance.

There is fossilized evidence of teocintle, the antecedent of what we know today as corn, growing in Oaxaca dating back more than eight thousand years, to what could have been the beginning of its domestication and that of other plants like beans, squash, and maguey (or agave, the plant from which mezcal is made).

The cultivation of corn, through a long process of selection and improvement carried out by our ancestors, made way for the milpa, the Mesoamerican agri-cultural technique that permits several crops to be planted on a single parcel of land, taking advantage of each one's particular features. In the milpa, corn, beans, and squash plants grow alongside each other, and later are combined in the cooking process. In this way, agriculture facilitated the emergence of vil-lages and then great civilizations, with corn the cornerstone of the Mesoameri-can diet, the legacy of which is still alive in Mexican kitchens today.

To paraphrase the Mexican ethnologist and anthropologist Guillermo Bonfil Batalla, corn is the foundation of Mexican culture, but it is also a realm of constant creativity. In Mexico we have more than forty species of said grain, as well as nixtamalization, the technique, invented in Oaxaca, by which grains are boiled with water and lime (calcium hydroxide), then rinsed and ground to form masa.

We Mexicans are, without doubt, men and women made of corn. We have cultivated our culture, our way of being in the world, alongside this plant.

Beyond its biology and its omnipresence in our food, corn is part of our social relationships and signals our strong link with the earth, each other, and beyond. It is found across agriculture, gastronomy, therapy, economy, politics, religion, and mythology in the daily life of small Mexican towns.

For all these reasons, a tortilla folded around anything is always a taco with history, and each bite gives us a taste of what we are.

MASA FROM LA RAYA DE ZIMATLÁN

The Nahua saying "Corn is our blood" is a reference to just how much of Mexican culture involves corn: it shows up on our dinner plates and in our religion.

Masa made of dried, nixtamalized corn is one of the most ancient food preparation methods to be found in Mesoamerica. Masa is essential for making memelas (page 14), tortillas (page 11), tamales (pages 41 and 45), and many other foods that have their origins in the pre-Hispanic world. These dishes may accompany a main course or be served as snacks, stuffed or covered with beans, pork asiento (lard and the crispy bits left over when making chicharrones), crema, beef, chicken, or pork, or bathed in salsa and dusted with cheese, cabbage, and herbs.

Makes 3 pounds of masa

Time: 2 to 4 hours

½ cup lime (also known as slaked lime, calcium hydroxide, or cal)

1 gallon water, plus more as needed

2 pounds dried heirloom corn (dried field corn)

Dissolve the lime in a large nonreactive pot with 1 gallon of water. (It might not all dissolve.) Make sure not to touch the lime with your bare hand as it can cause burns. Add the corn and place the pot over high heat. Once it begins to boil, lower the heat to medium and cook for about one hour, making sure there's always at least one inch of water covering the kernels. Timing will vary depending on corn variety and freshness. To check that the corn is ready, take a kernel and bite into it. The corn should feel soft on the outside, and a dot of white starch should be visible in the center.

Remove the pot from the heat, drain the cooking water, and add enough fresh water to cover the corn completely. Swish the kernels around and repeat a couple of times to rinse the corn well.

There are several options for grinding the corn: take it to a mill, grind it with a metate (the traditional tool used for making masa), or use a food processor. When using a food processor, grind in batches. Start with 2 cups of hydrated corn, and add water one tablespoon at a time as needed to help process the corn. Stop to scrape down the sides as you go. The dough is ready when no large pieces of corn remain. The resulting product is corn masa.

Note The texture of the masa should be soft and as moist as possible without sticking to your hands. If the masa cracks when you press it,

(recipe continues)

that means it's too dry. Correct this by adding water by the spoonful and kneading the masa until it is uniform and malleable. Making masa in a food processor might result in wetter masa, so be careful to add just enough water to keep the processor going. It is best to keep the masa covered with a damp cloth while it is being used. Masa is best used the day it's made, but can be tightly wrapped in plastic and refrigerated for up to three days.

TORTILLAS

In Mexico, you can still find mills where you can take nixtamalized corn to be ground. However, the most common way to purchase masa nowadays is from tortilla vendors. Tortillas can also be made with masa harina from popular brands such as Minsa or Maseca. The best quality masa is made with corn that has been recently nixtamalized and then ground—not from dry corn flour. If you are buying masa rather than making it yourself, try to get masa blanca, which is made from heirloom corn.

Tirar tortillas—to "throw" them, as the action is commonly called—takes more practice than dexterity. Once you have the masa, make a single tortilla to test that your dough has the right consistency. You want your masa to be soft and moist but not stick to your hands. If your masa is too wet, add masa harina by the spoonful until you achieve the desired consistency. If your masa is too dry, add water by the spoonful.

The best tortilla is always the most freshly made one. However, both tortillas and masa can be frozen. Masa is best used the day it's made, but can be tightly wrapped in plastic and refrigerated for up to three days.

Makes 2 dozen tortillas
Time: 45 minutes

1 pound of masa
  (page 8)

To make tortillas, you will need a tortilla press (or rolling pin) and two plastic sheets cut into squares or circles that are large enough to extend at least 2 inches beyond the diameter of the press. In Mexico, these sheets, known as "nylons," are normally made from plastic grocery bags. There are also those who press tortillas by hand, but that requires a lot of practice.

Preheat a comal, griddle, or well-seasoned cast-iron skillet over medium heat. Pinch off a small amount of masa, and roll it between your hands into a ball about 1½ to 2 inches wide. Place a plastic sheet over the bottom half of the tortilla press and put the masa ball on top of it, setting it slightly off-center (more toward the front of the press). Place the second plastic sheet over the ball, close, and press. Flatten the masa to about 1/16 inch. In order to give the tortilla an even thickness, turn the plastic sheets with the tortilla in it 180°, then exert pressure again. Hold the plastic with the tortilla still inside it in one hand and gently remove the top sheet. If the masa is the right consistency it should peel away easily. Remove the second sheet of plastic, and carefully place the tortilla on

(recipe continues)

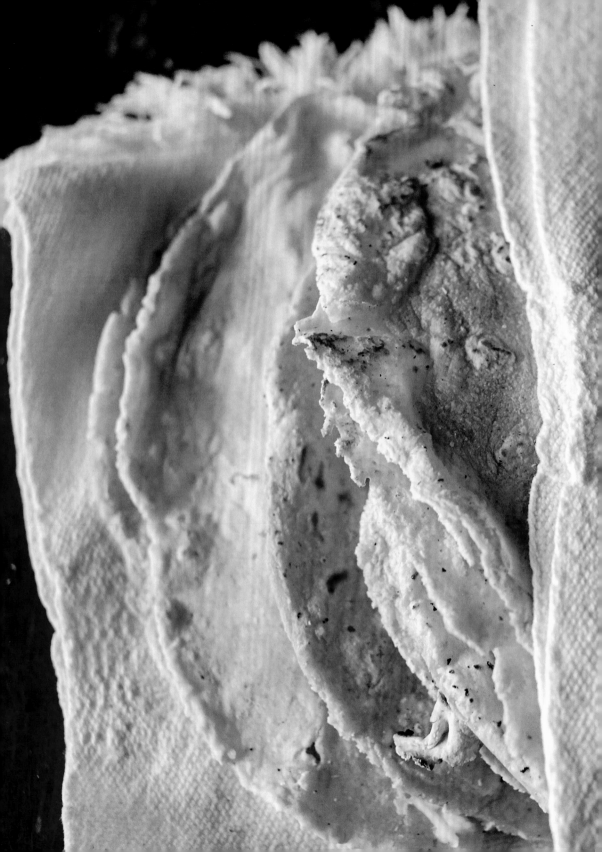

the hot comal, griddle, or skillet. After a few seconds, when the edges of the tortilla begin to dry out and the color lightens, turn the tortilla over. You can tap the tortilla a few times in the center, using two fingertips. This friction allows hot steam to enter and helps the tortilla cook more evenly. After another 20 or 30 seconds the tortilla might balloon. Turn it over a third time on the comal, griddle, or skillet, and cook for another 10 seconds. The side that is now facing up is called the cara, or the tortilla's "face."

Note Each tortilla should take around one full minute to cook. It is ready when both sides look dry, with some browned spots, yet is still moist and pliable. Once the tortillas are ready, wrap them in a clean dish towel to keep them warm.

MEMELAS

Memelas, thick corn masa cakes that are toasted on a comal, are just one of several similar masa preparations, including sopes (which are circular) or huaraches (which are oval-shaped). What sets memelas apart is their pinched edges and the use of pork asiento, or unrefined lard, which gives them an intense, extraordinary flavor.

Makes 35 memelas

Time: 1 hour

2 pounds corn masa (page 8)

¾ cup pork asiento (you may substitute lard, although the flavor will be a little different)

1 cup refried bean paste (page 40)

¾ cup crumbled queso fresco (or feta cheese)

Chile de agua salsa (page 17) or chile morita and miltomate salsa (page 53)

Preheat a comal, griddle, or a well-seasoned cast-iron skillet over medium heat. You will also need a tortilla press (or a rolling pin) and two pieces of plastic sheets cut into squares or circles that are large enough to extend at least 2 inches beyond the diameter of the press. Repurposed plastic grocery bags work well.

Take enough masa to roll into a small ball approximately 1½ inches in diameter, then reshape the masa into a log about 5 inches long, with the ends slightly tapered.

To form the memela, place the log between the two plastic sheets, and put it in the press. Close the press, and flatten the masa to about ⅛ inch. In order to give the memelas an even thickness, turn the plastic sheets around 180° and exert pressure again. You should end up with a 5½-by-3-inch oval.

Place the memela on the comal or pan, and cook for about 30 seconds. Turn it over, and cook for another 20 seconds. Flip the memela over once more and cook for another 15 seconds. The memela is done when the masa looks dry but still plump, not cracked. Remove from the comal or pan, and while still hot, use your thumb and index finger to pinch around the border of the memela, forming a lip.

Once all the memelas are formed, spread onto each one a teaspoon of pork asiento and a good amount of refried bean paste. Sprinkle with the cheese, and return the memelas to the comal or pan to lightly toast the bottoms. Serve warm with chile de agua salsa or any other salsa of your choice.

CHILE DE AGUA SALSA

In La Raya de Zimatlán, where I was born, while memelas are prepared on the comal, chiles de agua and heirloom tomatoes are placed on the embers to roast, taking advantage of the same fire. These are acidic, sweet, fresh-flavored ingredients native to the region: there couldn't be a simpler, more Oaxacan salsa than this. It's an ideal accompaniment for memelas. If you cannot find chiles de agua, substitute Anaheim, jalapeño, or chilaca chiles instead.

Serves 4

Time: 20 minutes

1 chile de agua, stemmed and deveined (or substitute Anaheim, jalapeño, or chilaca chiles)

2 tomatoes

1 small clove garlic or half a medium-sized clove

½ tablespoon salt

Set a comal, pan, or cast-iron skillet over high heat. Roast the chiles and the tomatoes, turning them over occasionally until their skin is partly charred and they are soft to the touch. The chiles will be done first. It'll take about 5 to 10 minutes for the tomatoes.

Rub the garlic along the walls of a molcajete, discarding the rest. If using a mortar and pestle instead, pound only half the raw garlic clove into a paste. Then add the chile, pound some more, and follow with the tomatoes. You don't want to completely disintegrate the chile and tomatoes, you are looking for a chunky consistency. Add salt and mix well.

CHRONICLE OF A FIESTA

It's ten in the morning and I've arrived at the garden. About half a mile north of La Raya de Zimatlán lies the plot of land where I decided to develop a garden to supply my restaurants. Here is where we'll have a party, what is known around these parts as a mayordomía. A celebration for my loved ones that includes a banquet, music, and mezcal. A mayordomía can happen for any number of reasons: to celebrate a wedding, the feast of a patron saint, or for no reason at all—just to cut loose, just for the heck of it, just because life has been kind.

Today, I went early to the Mercado de Abastos in Oaxaca city to buy all the ingredients that wouldn't be available at the garden, such as serving dishes, papel picado decorations, and flowers. Then we stopped to pick up my aunts at their house. There are many chickens, two cows, and a few still young piglets at the lot. There is corn dried for the season and my aunts are armed with all kinds of supplies to prepare the meal. Meche, Raquel, and Chalina will be the head cooks. Don Rafael and Doña Isabel, my grandparents, join the committee, knowing there's not a minute to lose when there's a party.

In the span of forty-eight hours we will have prepared and consumed the most emblematic dishes, not just of this region of Oaxaca, but of my childhood. These dishes are my birthright.

The first day in the garden is a day for preparations, but that doesn't mean that we aren't celebrating already. The festivities begin with the planning, the buying of ingredients, the harvest, and the picking. My cousins work, building a tapesco (a grill) and a roof; Uncle Sergio cuts herbs for the different recipes we're going to make. Aunts Meche, Raquel, and Chalina start the fire and then prepare the coffee, chocolate, and champurrado (a chocolate drink). Before continuing, we must have breakfast, pan dulce (Mexican pastries), memelas, and more.

Aunt Raquel cures the comales—the griddles—with lime. Cousin Peluche goes to a neighboring milpa to gather the ingredients for the sopa de guías (page 35). Aunt Meche directs us as we work to cut up the squash, the guías (the runners) and the blossoms, to clean herbs like chepiche and hierba de conejo (an herb with an earthy, aniselike aroma), and to slice fresh corn cobs, while the other women stay by the fire to begin preparing the most elemental ingredient for the meal: the nixtamalized corn that will be the base of tamales and tortillas.

This is how we will spend the next two days: working, eating, cooking, and enjoying each other's company. The women communicate in silence, consulting one another with quick glances, answering in kind with a look, or beginning to stir the pot or fan the fire, as if the signal had been direct. Here, to learn, you have to pay attention.

The chigol—the person who serves the mezcal—dutifully ensures that all those who arrive to help, or to have breakfast or lunch, drink their helpings a little at a time. This ancestral beverage is the fuel that keeps the action going. It is the spirit that gives this work its soul.

Every once in a while, the cooks meet eyes with the chigol, because the work must go on, and for that to happen sustenance is needed. Cousin Zenaida and Aunt Clemencia have joined the team, their hands helping at the metate, washing dishes, and friends Peluche and Diego are headed to town in case anyone needs something. They'll give the cooks a ride to take the mole negro ingredients—now charred—to the mill, and bring back firewood. Other cousins are arriving to drink a beer, eat a tamalito, smaller than the traditional tamale, or have a memela (page 14).

The stage is set. The brass band arrives, the papel picado decorations are hung, the pots are moved, the agua fresca is made, the dishes are washed, and more mezcal, more beer, and more food are served. After sharing breakfast, now we are also sharing the music, the laughter, the warmth of all the hours of working and drinking together.

The moment arrives for all to sit down: now it is time to try the sopa de guías and the mole. All is silent for a spell. The earth smells wet and the air is clean. In the distance, we can see a team of oxen. Here, at the long tables, we are all content. The flavors are like a promise fulfilled. The embers, the earth, the herbs, we have seen it all, smelled it all, touched it as it transformed, and now everything makes sense in our mouths. It was done as it should be done, and it tastes as it should taste. There is a freshness and an authenticity that cannot be faked; there is an affection and a care taken with this meal that cannot be hidden.

My aunts do not eat until the rest of us have eaten, they are vigilant, proud of what they have offered us. They can read upon our faces that their goals have been achieved. With that satisfaction, they can now sit at the table and receive well-deserved praise and much needed mezcal. They have nourished us with the fire, with their own hands.

At the fiesta in La Raya there has been no order, but rather cycles in which things are done. The chigol must continue serving mezcal and drinking it with everyone, to honor their presence, to honor life. The band must strike back up with "Pinotepa." The aroma of smoke, the vision of the fire, and the flavor of the mole will last. The music closes the cycle, the time has come to sing the verses, the time has come to dance, to laugh. We are joined together by all of our senses.

MOLOTES WITH POTATO AND CHORIZO

To make the molotes, mix the corn masa and corn starch in a bowl, adding water as needed until you have a mixture that is smooth and even but not sticky. Season with salt to taste. Set aside.

Heat 4 tablespoons of the vegetable oil in a pan, then fry the chorizo for about five minutes. Add the onion and continue to cook over medium heat until the onions caramelize. Add the potato and mix well. Season with salt to taste. Set aside.

To make the guacamole, coarsely mash the avocados, then add the onion, cilantro, and salt, and mix well.

To make the salsa, place all the ingredients in a blender and blend with ½ cup water until smooth. Season with salt.

To assemble the molotes, take approximately 2 tablespoons of the prepared masa at a time and roll each into a balls. Flatten them, as for tortillas, between two sheets of plastic using a tortilla press or rolling pin. Working carefully, fill the flattened ball with a small amount of the potato and chorizo mixture, and roll it into a sealed cylinder. Make sure there are no holes in the masa, and that the ends are closed or pinched shut, as leaking can cause the molotes to explode while frying. Let them rest in the refrigerator for an hour. Heat 2 cups vegetable oil in a deep pot over medium-high heat until it shimmers and a small piece of masa dropped into it starts frying and bubbling right away. Fry the molotes a few at a time in the hot oil. Avoid crowding the pot. Turn them over constantly as they fry, until they are golden brown, then remove them to paper towels or a rack to drain.

Serve with the guacamole and salsa.

Serves 4

Time: 1 hour

For the molotes

1 pound corn masa (page 8)

3½ ounces corn starch

Water as needed

Salt, to taste

4 tablespoons vegetable oil, for the filling, plus 2 cups for frying the molotes

7 ounces pork chorizo, crumbled

¼ white onion, finely chopped

7 ounces potato (about 1 medium potato), boiled and coarsely mashed

For the guacamole

1 avocado

1 ounce white onion, chopped

1 tablespoon cilantro, chopped

Salt, to taste

For the salsa

3 chiles de árbol, lightly toasted

3 guajillo chiles, lightly toasted

2 cloves raw garlic

½ cup water

Salt, to taste

LOOMS OF CACAO

The mountainous landscape around Mitla, an archaeological site about thirty miles southeast of Oaxaca city, conceals numerous caves that have existed for thousands of years: caves that served as dens, refuges, or sacred sites connected to deities and forces of nature with whom ancient and current Zapotec residents maintain communication.

One of these is called the Devil's Cave, a great hollow that leads to a site filled with ritual items that have been deposited there over time. Candles, bird feathers, parcels tied with string, wilted flowers, and infinite quantities of cacao. Those who live here say that cacao is payment to the gods, just as it was in times of old: the currency offered in exchange for their favor.

Cacao is a beloved piece of our culture—our first currency, a medicine to protect against heart attacks and, once transformed into hot chocolate, the magic beverage of which Moctezuma drank up to seventeen cups a day.

At various sites in Oaxaca, when a wedding date draws near, tradition calls for around 100 pounds of cacao to be ground with cinnamon and sugar. The evening before the ceremony, women gather with their metates to grind and to form the spheres of chocolate that will be given as favors to the wedding party and the family members of the bride and groom. A cup of hot chocolate is also the first beverage offered to all the guests at a wedding, together with pan dulce made with egg yolks, a snack that marks the beginning of the festivities.

Petrona Vicente, a Zapotec woman from Teotitlán del Valle, wears thick braids threaded with ribbons that wrap around her head, forming a kind of celestial headpiece. Every morning she sits behind a metate acquired in 1946 and prepares the cacao beans, the cinnamon, and the sugar to be ground. To grind is a laborious task that requires perfect knowledge of how to use the metate—training that began, in earlier times, at the tender age of eight. Petrona treasures the different metates on her patio, on which she grinds not only chocolate, but corn, chiles, pastes for mole, cochineal, indigo, and various herbs to produce the dyes she employs in making wool rugs.

Each morning she grinds the chocolate she herself will drink, and she heats the water on the stove. When it boils, she submerges the balls of chocolate, which, with the help of a molinillo, a hand-carved, wooden, whisk-like kitchen tool used for frothing hot chocolate, will become the coveted foam that brings forth the same smile, day after day. Her chocolate is of high quality. Petrona, who has drunk a cup of hot chocolate every day at sunrise since she was small, empties it into a cup and sips it slowly, silently.

To grind and to weave are her trades. She grinds her morning nourishment and she grinds the dyes that imprint their colors on the wool threads she later weaves together under a burning sun whose rays push into the open-air hallway of her house. When I see her cacao-dyed hands slide over the metate, I can't help but think that to grind is also to weave, to combine substances, to thread together not threads but flavors.

In Oaxaca, cacao beans have born witness to deep social, economic, and familial relationships. For that reason, whether whole, broken, ground, or mixed, they are vessels that communicate our culture. A cup of hot chocolate is a work of art which, when drunk, is woven into the deepest parts of our being, like the weavings of cacao piled on the floors of so many caves, to remind us of the different ways we eat and drink together.

ATOLE BLANCO

Atole is a hot, thick drink made from cooked, ground corn that is diluted with water. Depending on the region, and the type of corn, how it's made or flavored may vary. It can be sweet, sour, spicy, or savory, although savory atoles are considered more a stew than a drink. The basic atole, or white atole, is a smooth canvas that can be flavored with fruit, nuts, and spices, and sweetened with sugar, piloncillo (unrefined cane sugar), or honey. Although it is present at ceremonies and rituals alike, it has been considered a drink of the poor, unlike chocolate, which at one time was exclusively consumed by high-ranking figures. It's a comforting popular beverage throughout Mexico that is often served next to tamales for breakfast, as a snack, at parties, or for dinner.

Makes 8 cups
Time: 1 hour 30 minutes

1 pound dried white corn
½ gallon plus 4 cups water

In a large pot, boil the corn in ½ gallon of water for about an hour or until the corn breaks apart when you scratch it with your fingernail. The time it will take depends on a number of factors, including how fresh the corn is and the type of vessel it's cooked in. Remove from heat and set aside to cool. Working in batches, purée in a blender along with the water in which it was boiled. Once all the corn is pureed, add 4 cups of water to dilute it.

Using cheesecloth or a fine mesh sieve, strain into a large saucepan, discarding the solids. Boil over medium heat, stirring constantly with a wooden spoon, for about 15 minutes or until the mixture thickens. The time you cook it will depend on the consistency you like your atole. More cooking time will yield a thicker mixture (a bit less dense than porridge), and less time, a thinner beverage that is easily poured.

Note In Oaxaca atole is consumed hot or cold, with hojaldra, a type of rustic pan dulce dusted with red-dyed sugar.

CHAMPURRADO

If you can't find Oaxacan chocolate, try substituting with an equal amount of semi-sweet chocolate, and add 1½ teaspoons cinnamon powder and 1 drop of almond extract.

———————————

In a large pot, boil the corn with 8 cups water for about an hour or until the corn breaks apart when you scratch it with your fingernail. The time this will take depends on a number of factors, including how fresh the corn is and the type of vessel it's cooked in. Remove from heat and set aside to cool. Working in batches, purée in a blender along with the water in which it was boiled. Once all the corn is pureed, add 4 cups of water to dilute it.

Using cheesecloth or a fine mesh sieve, strain into a large saucepan, discarding the solids. Add the chocolate and sugar and boil over medium heat, stirring constantly with a wooden spoon, until the chocolate melts and the sugar dissolves.

Makes 8 cups

Time: 1 hour 30 minutes

1 pound dried white corn

8 cups plus 4 cups water

1½ cups shaved Oaxacan chocolate

¼ cup sugar

MAYORDOMÍAS: HOSTING AS A CELEBRATION

In Oaxaca, mayordomías are celebrations of saints' feast days and other sig-
nificant dates on the calendar of the Catholic Church. They entail festive pro-
ductions on an immense scale. To be a mayordomo, or head of the festivity, is
to take on a responsibility that includes entertaining family, friends, neighbors,
and other community members.

Mayordomías require the participation of many people with different talents
and abilities. For this reason a mayordomo is never alone and invites guests well
ahead of time, looking to secure the work and help that will later be necessary.
This is why mayordomías are celebrations that not only fill the belly, but also
feed social relationships and build and strengthen the community.

At many celebrations, food is often prepared not only for the guests, but also
for the dead, mythical deities, Catholic saints, and for its atmospheric powers.
Offerings to the dead may be the most well-known example of this practice,
but they are not its only expression. In this way, food plays a central role in the
religious and ceremonial life of the town.

Special preparations of moles, soups, tamales, and other assorted dishes
testify to the different seasons of the year, the relationship to the environment,
the availability of local products, and the search for that which comes from afar.
Meanwhile, in kitchens, a multitude of hands (which are usually female) inter-
weave in close coordination to make food en masse, with the ultimate purpose
of sharing a meal and creating a collective gathering.

The offerings with their candles, flowers, and dressed-up saints, together
with music, papel picado decorations, and multicolored clay plates upon long
tables laden with corn-based drinks, beer, and mezcal, are the salt and pepper
that season our celebrations.

SOPA DE GUÍAS

This soup is made in the rainy season, in August or September, when the corn plants yield their cobs. All of the ingredients that you need for this recipe—piojito, chepil, squash blossoms, calabacita güichi, and chepiche—grow in that season, either in the milpa or in the surrounding hills. This dish requires the family to come together into the fields. The preparation is collective: some people clean herbs, others chop, others shuck corn. It is a special occasion because it marks the first harvest, when the fields begin to give. It is an omen that sustenance will be provided.

_____

Bring ½ gallon of water plus 1 tablespoon of salt to a boil in a large pot. While the water boils, purée the garlic and the onion in a blender, along with ½ cup of water. Add the mixture to the boiling water, along with the sliced corn cobs and ground corn. Lower the heat to medium and cook until the liquid thickens, about 10 to 12 minutes. A white foam may rise to the surface; this is normal and can be removed with a spoon.

Once the broth has thickened, add the calabacita güichi or baby zucchini and let it cook for 5 minutes, or until it begins to soften and turn bright green. Add the guías and cook for another 5 minutes. Lastly, add the chepil, chepiche, piojito, and squash blossoms to the soup. Taste and add salt as desired. Serve as soon as possible so that the herbs retain their intense green color.

Serve with chile guajillo salsa (see page 36) to taste.

Notes

- This soup uses calabacita güichi, a different squash variety from the Támala or pumpkin squash. All the parts of the plant are used: the flower, the fruit, and the runners (the squash's thin climbing vines). If it's unavailable, you can substitute with baby zucchini.
- It is important to select the tenderest parts of the runners, as the thick branches closest to the roots are very fibrous.
- The easiest way to cut the corn into 1-inch-thick slices is to take a knife and place it over the corn where it should be cut, then hit it with a mallet or hammer.
- Sometimes this soup is thickened and enriched with masa or chochoyotes (small balls of masa) in addition to the ground corn. Before adding the chochoyotes to the soup, where they'll cook, a small indentation is made so that their bowl shape holds a small pool of broth.

Serves 6

Time: 1 hour 45 minutes (including time to clean and prepare the greens and herbs)

½ gallon plus ½ cup water

1 tablespoon salt, plus more, to taste

2 cloves garlic

¼ onion, roughly chopped

1 cob of corn, cut into 1-inch-thick slices

2 cups fresh corn, ground with ½ cup water

4 cups calabacita güichi or baby zucchini, cleaned and chopped into ½-inch pieces

1 cup guías de calabaza (or squash or pumpkin runners), cut into 1-inch-thick pieces

½ cup chepil leaves (or subsitute arugula or watercress)

2 tablespoons chepiche leaves, roughly chopped

½ cup hierba del piojito leaves, roughly chopped

1 cup squash blossoms, roughly chopped

CHILE GUAJILLO SALSA

Stem the chiles and roast them in a pan until their color changes and their smell intensifies, about 3 minutes. Remove from heat and pour ½ cup of water into the pan to rehydrate the chiles. Soak for a couple of minutes or until the skin has softened. In a blender, process the chiles along with the water, the garlic, and a teaspoon salt. When blending, add water by the tablespoon as needed to achieve a thick, smooth consistency. Strain before serving.

3 chiles guajillos
½ cup water
1 clove garlic
1 teaspoon salt

FRIJOLES DE LA OLLA

The fresher the beans, the faster they will cook. Soaking them overnight will also reduce the cooking time. A hard bean that was harvested some time ago can take up to 4 hours to cook. Frijoles de la olla may be refrigerated, but they turn sour easily, so should be boiled for a few minutes whenever you take them out of the fridge. I believe they improve as the days go by, as every time they are heated the liquid thickens and the flavor becomes more concentrated.

_____

To clean the beans, spread them out and discard any small stones and bits of debris. Rinse them a couple of times and allow to soak overnight, making sure they are covered with water by at least 2 inches.

Drain and rinse the beans, and place them in a pot with about ½ gallon of water, or enough to cover by 1 inch. Add the onion and garlic and bring to a boil. Reduce heat to medium-low, and let the beans simmer for approximately 2 hours, stirring occasionally. The beans should always be covered by about 1 inch of water, so add additional hot water as necessary.

The beans are ready when you can see their skin has split and a single bean can be squished between your fingers. At this point, add the epazote and salt and let them cook for 15 to 20 minutes more.

Serves 12 (makes about 4 pounds)

Time: 12 hours (or overnight) to soak and 3 hours to cook

2 pounds frijol delgado negro, or dried black beans

Water to cover plus ½ gallon water

1 medium onion, cut in half

1 head garlic, cut in half crosswise

2 stems of fresh epazote (or dried, if fresh is not available)

1 tablespoon salt

BEAN PASTE

This can be made without the aromatics (avocado leaves and epazote). You will miss out on some of the distinctive flavor but still get good results.

Serves 12 (makes about 4 pounds)
Time: 30 minutes

1 onion, chopped into wedges

2 cloves garlic, smashed

1 stem of epazote, whole (or dried, if fresh is not available)

¼ cup lard

1 chile de árbol, slightly charred

3 avocado leaves, slightly charred

Salt, to taste

To make the bean paste, follow the recipe for frijoles de la olla (page 39) and reserve 1 cup of the cooked bean broth. Then, fry the onion, garlic, and epazote in a pan with the lard. Once the ingredients begin to caramelize and burn slightly at the edges, remove from the heat and discard all but the flavored lard, reserving it in the pan.

Transfer the beans to a blender in batches and purée with their liquid, the chile de árbol, and the avocado leaves. Add water as needed in order to blend completely, and arrive at a smooth paste.

Fry the black bean purée in the pan with the flavored lard, stirring occasionally to avoid burning. The water will slowly evaporate and the beans will dry into a paste. You will know it's done when a spoon dragged across the bottom of the pan leaves a trail. Taste for salt and adjust as desired.

BEAN TAMALES

This recipe is made with good-quality fresh masa, which is why it doesn't call for much liquid. If you make the recipe from packaged masa harina, you can use chicken, beef, or vegetable stock rather than plain water. The miltomate water used here has leavening properties which result in a fluffier tamal.

If using commercially sold masa harina, follow the instructions on the packaging and then continue with shaping the tamales.

If you cannot find hoja santa, the tamales can be prepared without it.

Makes 20 tamales

Time: 3 hours

2 pounds fresh masa

½ cup agua de hoja de miltomate (tomatillo water) (page 45)

¾ cup whipped lard (lightly whipping the lard makes for an airy tamal)

1 tablespoon salt

30 corn husks, rinsed and soaked in warm water for 20 minutes

10 to 20 hoja santa leaves (depending on their size), stems removed (if the leaf is very large, cut it up and use one piece per tamal)

2 cups bean paste (page 40)

Mix the masa with the agua de hoja de miltomate, lard, and salt and knead for 20 to 30 minutes. You can do this in a stand mixer with the paddle attachment and it will take about half the time. The purpose of kneading (or batido, whipping) the dough is to incorporate air. When the masa looks glossy and feels fluffier, take a piece of dough and drop it into a glass of cold water; if the dough floats, the masa is ready. Cover the masa with plastic wrap or a damp cloth and let it rest for an hour.

To shape the tamales, take a totomoxtle or husk, holding the base of the leaf against the palm of your hand, and leaving the pointy end toward your fingertips. Take two tablespoons of masa and spread it over the husk, from the middle downward. Cover the right side all the way to the edge, but leave about an inch clear on the left side. Take an hoja santa leaf (or a piece of a leaf if they are very large) and set it in the middle of the masa. Place a heaping tablespoon of bean paste over the hoja santa. To wrap the tamal, fold the right side of the husk over the filling, then fold the left side over to cover, and finally fold the narrow tip of the husk down. You'll end up with a square-ish tamal. Set it aside and continue until all the tamales are shaped.

To cook the tamales, place them in a steamer forming a spiral pattern. The wide side of the totomoxtle should be facing up. Make sure to leave enough space between them so that steam can circulate freely, as this will help the tamales cook evenly. Some people like to place a coin in the bottom of the pot; this way, it rattles as the water boils. If it goes quiet, it means more hot water needs to be added.

(recipe continues)

Once all the tamales are in the steamer, cover them with a damp cloth, then cover with the lid. Cook for 30 to 35 minutes. Turn off heat, and let sit for 5 minutes before removing the lid and testing for doneness. Cooking time will depend on the size of your tamales and how they're set up in the pot. The tamal is done when the dough has turned darker and less opaque, and the husk easily pulls away from the tamal.

CHEPIL TAMALES

Chepil tamales are traditionally prepared in the rainy season. They are characterized by the inclusion of maíz quebrado (broken corn), which gives them a grainier texture. Chepil is a nutritious, flavorful wild herb that is used in soups, salads, and tamales in the Mexican states of Oaxaca, Veracruz, and Chiapas.

———————————

To make the agua de hoja de miltomate, place the husks and 2 cups water in a small pot over medium heat. It's okay if the water does not cover the husks completely. Bring to a boil and cook, stirring occasionally, for about 15 minutes. Strain and reserve the water.

To make the tamal dough, place the corn kernels in a pot with enough water to cover them by 1 inch. Boil until they are soft on the outside but still show an uncooked spot in the center, about 2 to 3 hours. The time will vary depending on how old and dry the kernels are. Make sure that the corn is covered by at least 1 inch of water at all times. Drain and set aside to cool.

In the meantime, pick the chepil leaves from their stems and set aside. Be sure to pick only the leaves, as the stem is very tough.

Place the cooled corn into a food processor, and using the pulse button, grind until no large pieces remain. Slowly add the miltomate water and process some more, until you arrive at a grainy paste. Scrape down the sides of the processor as needed to get a homogenous texture.

Transfer the corn paste to a bowl along with the corn masa and knead to combine. Mix in the salt and lard and knead for 20 to 30 minutes. You can do this in a stand mixer with the paddle attachment; it will take about 15 minutes. Finally, add the chepil and knead by hand until incorporated. The purpose of kneading (or batido, whipping) the dough is to incorporate air. When the masa looks glossy and feels fluffier, take a piece of dough and drop it into a glass of cold water; if the dough floats, the masa is ready. Cover the masa with plastic wrap or a damp cloth and let it rest for an hour.

To shape the tamales, take a corn husk, holding the base of the leaf against the palm of your hand, and leaving the pointy end toward your

(recipe continues)

Makes 20 tamales

Time: 3 hours

For the agua de hoja de miltomate (tomatillo water)

10 miltomate or tomatillo husks

2 cups water

For the tamales

2 cups dried corn kernels (preferably white heirloom corn)

Water to cover

½ cup chepil leaves (or substitute arugula or watercress)

½ cup agua de hoja de miltomate (see above)

1 pound corn masa (homemade or from a tortillería)

1½ tablespoons salt

¾ cup lard

30 corn husks, soaked in warm water for 10 minutes

fingertips. Take two heaping tablespoons of masa and spread it over the husk, from the middle downward. Cover the right side all the way to the edge, but leave about an inch clear on the left side. To wrap the tamal, fold the right side of the husk over the filling, then fold the left side over to cover, and finally fold the narrow tip of the husk down. You'll end up with a somewhat squared-out tamal. Set it aside and continue until all the tamales are shaped.

To cook the tamales, place them in a steamer forming a spiral pattern. The wide side of the husk should be facing up. Make sure to leave enough space between them so that steam can circulate freely, as this will help the tamales cook evenly. Some people like to place a coin in the bottom of the pot; this way, it rattles as the water boils. If it goes quiet, it means more hot water needs to be added.

Once all the tamales are in the steamer, cover them with a damp cloth. Cook for 30 to 35 minutes. Turn off heat, and let sit for 5 minutes before removing the lid and testing for doneness. Cooking time will depend on the size of your tamales and how they're set up in the pot. The tamal is done when the dough has turned darker and less opaque, and the husk easily pulls away from the tamal.

THERE'S NO CELEBRATION WITHOUT SEGUEZA

Segueza is one of the traditional dishes prepared for special occasions in the central valley region of Oaxaca. It is characteristically served at weddings or fandangos, as marriage festivities are called in this area, which last anywhere from three to five days. As with all Oaxacan parties, the food and drink are the stars of a wedding celebration, and great importance is bestowed on the cooks.

There are many foods prepared for these occasions, among them chicken livers, hot chocolate with pan dulce, mole negro (page 57), and, of course, segueza. In addition, a few days before the events, a party favor or cariño is given to members of the family and the wedding party, consisting of a basket with great quantities of chocolate, pan dulce (pan de resobado, pan de yema, pan marquesote), fruits, and, often, prepared dishes.

The word "segueza" has ancient origins. According to residents of Teotitlán del Valle, it comes from the Zapotec words sa', meaning "party" or "celebration," and guè, which is the common name for atole, a corn-based drink served at the celebrations.

Generally segueza—a type of stew—is made with chicken, beef, or pork broth; toasted corn ground on a metate; a garlic paste also made on a metate; and chiles (guajillo, ancho, and red chilhuacle); with bits of asadura (offal) and hoja santa as condiments. It is always cooked in clay pots over a fogón, the improvised structure where a fire is made for cooking.

In Teotitlán, segueza is made with beans, and a dish known as segueza de amarillo is made with chicken broth and chile guajillo paste, prepared the day after the wedding with the broth that was used for the party.

Whatever the local style may call for, the preparation of segueza is quite elaborate, mostly for the time it takes to grind the toasted corn in the metate and then to cook it in abundant quantities. In fact, there are places where this dish is no longer made, because of its complexity.

As with every ritually prepared dish, there are myths that surround segueza. Grandmothers from Teotitlán say that if the beans don't cook quickly it's because the woman should not yet marry. In Xoxocotlán they say that the chiles must be ground when you're happy, because otherwise the dish will turn out very spicy.

As breakfast, as part of the main meal, or to enjoy the following day, segueza is the dish that everyone anxiously awaits at a wedding. That is why, in the valleys, they say there is no celebration without segueza, and no segueza without celebration.

SEGUEZA DE FANDANGO

Cook the pork ribs in the 8 cups of water, salted to taste, over medium heat for about 35 minutes, or until they are soft but firm. Remove the ribs, reserve the cooking liquid, and return the pot to the stove.

In a blender, blend the pepper, cumin, cloves, onion, garlic, chiles, and oregano with 2 cups of the reserved cooking liquid, then strain and add to the pot. Return the ribs to the pot, adding the hoja santa, and cook for 20 minutes over medium heat. Add the ground corn, stir until combined, and cook until the ground corn is soft, about 30 minutes. Add in more of the cooking liquid, up to 3 cups as needed as the corn soaks up liquid, to keep the segueza from drying out.

Season the segueza to taste, and serve.

Serves 4
Time 1½ hours

2¼ pounds pork ribs

8 cups water

Salt

5 black peppercorns, toasted

Pinch cumin, toasted

5 whole cloves, toasted

½ medium white onion, roasted

2 cloves garlic, roasted

6 guajillo chiles, seeds and veins removed, soaked in lukewarm water for 10 minutes

1 tablespoon oregano

4 hoja santa leaves

1¼ cups, or 7 ounces by weight, dry corn kernels, toasted in the oven at 535°F for 20 minutes, then coarsely ground in a blender

AGUA DE LEMONGRASS

Traditionally this infusion is prepared by grinding the lemongrass in a metate (a flat stone used for grinding), but you can also use a high-powered blender (the green part of the lemongrass stalk, which is essential for this recipe, can be pretty rough on a regular blender). If you are using a metate, to extract the juice, crush the plant from base to tip, adding water little by little until it becomes a pulp that is then mixed with sweetened water. Ground this way, the green color is more intense and the flavor even more refreshing.

Makes 1 quart

Time: 15 minutes

2 cups water, plus more as needed

1 bunch lemongrass stalks

¼ cup sugar

––––––––––––––––––

Bring 2 cups of water to a boil in a pot with the lemongrass and sugar. Boil for a couple of minutes to dissolve the sugar and let the leaves soften. Remove from the heat.

Once cool, chop the lemongrass into pieces and blend in a blender along with the water in which it boiled. Strain through a sieve covered with a dish towel or fine cheesecloth.

Add enough water to reach 1 quart.

Serve with plenty of ice.

CHILE MORITA AND MILTOMATE SALSA

Chiles morita are roasted and smoked jalapeños. This chile's burnt-wood flavor, together with the acid from the miltomates (tomatillos) makes for a salsa that covers the entire palate.

Traditionally salsa is made in a molcajete (a mortar made of volcanic stone), using a tejolote (a stone pestle) to crush the ingredients. Usually molcajetes are carved from volcanic stone, which contributes to the flavor of the salsa. But if a molcajete is not available a blender can be used instead.

Serves 4
Time: 20 minutes

3 chiles morita
5 miltomates or tomatillos
1 clove garlic
½ tablespoon salt
1 tablespoon onion, diced
1 tablespoon chopped cilantro

———————————————

Set a comal, pan, or cast-iron skillet over high heat.

Roast the chiles, turning over once, until they inflate and their color changes to a deep red or brown, about 2 minutes. Take care not to burn them, as that will make the salsa bitter. You can roast the miltomates alongside the chiles, turning them over occasionally until their skin is partly charred and they are soft to the touch, about 5 to 10 minutes.

If using a molcajete, place garlic and salt inside and grind with the tejolote until a paste is formed. Add the chiles and grind until they are mostly crushed. Add the miltomates and pound some more until everything is incorporated but your salsa is still chunky. If using a blender, first use a knife to make a paste of garlic and salt by finely chopping the garlic then incorporating the salt, and crushing the garlic between the blade of your knife and the cutting board. Place the garlic paste, chiles, and miltomates into a blender, in this order. Process, turning the blender on and off, in short bursts, as you don't want to purée the salsa. You are looking for some bigger pieces of miltomate and chiles here and there.

Mix in the chopped onion and cilantro using a spoon.

Because miltomates are high in pectin, the sauce might be thick. If so, add a drizzle of water and taste for salt. This salsa is an excellent condiment for ceviche tostadas and quesadillas.

THE COLOR OF THE EARTH

There is a place where you can make a stew that is green, thick, and acidic, made with local miltomates (an heirloom variety of tomatillo), soledad chiles, and chiles de agua, native herbs, and aromatic hoja santa picked from the back garden. It is traditionally served in earthenware that is also green and enjoyed on a patio that reflects the green hues of the cantera stone that gave the city its first name: Antequera.

That place is Oaxaca; the state with the greatest biological and cultural diversity in all of Mexico, with more than twenty-five endemic species of chiles growing from the coast to the mountains and the valleys: chilhuacles, pasillas, chiles de agua, and more, in shades of green, yellow, copper, black, and maroon, like the different colors of earth found throughout the state.

If you look out the window on the highway that leads to Oaxaca state, you'll be submerged in a colorful dream of different earthen tones, adorned with mountains, organ pipe cacti, and skies that are always blue, bordering the country of the clouds.

Just as the roads are covered with specific mixes of minerals that we tread upon as we walk, just as potters make pastes with these same minerals in order to offer us more colorful ceramics, in this way the earth gives us chiles, seeds, and ingredients that metates, molcajetes, and human hands convert into edible pastes that we call moles.

Clays and moles give color and flavor to the creations of those who make ceramics and those who make guisos (stews), those whose art makes use of their knowledge of mixture, cooking, and precise timing.

These guisos—estofados, coloraditos, amarillos, verdes, negros, manchamanteles, and chichilos—tell the stories of weddings, births, parties, and other events that are part of the cycle of daily and ritual life. They speak their specific techniques for preparation, service, and consumption. They are the abstraction of insight bequeathed by word of mouth throughout history.

Oaxacan moles and the ceramics that hold them are a metaphor that potters and cooks put on our tables, alchemies concocted over low heat, a still intact allegory of our spicy earth.

MOLE NEGRO

People often think of making mole as a complicated process, but the truth is that while it's labor-intensive, it's not complex. Making mole requires more patience than dexterity. Charring each of the ingredients over a comal or griddle, tossing them from side to side, and observing their transformation, can even become a contemplative act. The complexity is found in the flavor, not in the preparation. Mole is the premier celebratory sauce in Oaxaca for weddings, mayordomías, saints' feasts, and social gatherings in general.

The color and flavor of mole negro comes from the degree to which the ingredients are toasted, since they are charred on the comal until they turn black. The recipe shown here is for making a mole paste. To serve, add stock. The mole flavor will evolve with time, so the paste benefits from being made in advance.

Before you begin, make sure you have all your ingredients ready. Dry chiles should always be cleaned with a damp kitchen towel before being used. Preheat a comal or a well-seasoned cast-iron skillet or griddle. Stem and devein all the chiles and reserve their seeds. Have a large bowl on hand. You can place each ingredient there after you've browned it, as later on they'll all be processed together.

Toast the chiles over medium heat for about 12 minutes, or until they are charred and black. Set them aside. Now, toast the chile seeds for 8 to 10 minutes, and set them aside. In the same pan, roast the garlic, onion, and tomatoes until charred in parts, and set them aside. Toast the herbs, spices, nuts, and sesame seeds and set aside. You are looking to lightly brown each ingredient and bring out its aroma. Add a tablespoon of lard to the pan and fry the raisins and prunes until plump, about 1 minute. Fry the pan amarillito until golden. Reserve everything in the bowl as you go.

Traditionally, the unpeeled plantains are placed directly over the embers, until their skin chars and the flesh caramelizes. To obtain similar results, roast the unpeeled plantain in the pan or griddle. Cook, turning the plantain over occasionally until it softens and the skin is burnt. Allow to cool, then peel it, and place it in the bowl.

(recipe continues)

Makes 1 pound mole paste

Time: 2 hours 30 minutes

3 chiles chilhuacle (if you cannot find chiles chilhuacle, use additional chiles pasilla, ancho, negro, mulato, or meco)

3 chiles pasilla

3 chiles ancho, negro, or mulato

2 chiles meco

3 cloves garlic, sliced

½ medium-sized onion, cut into wedges

3 tomatoes (4 if they are small), preferably guajillo or Roma

½ tablespoon dried thyme

½ tablespoon dried marjoram

½ tablespoon dried rosemary

1 tablespoon dried oregano

4 whole cloves

5 allspice berries

1 pinch anise seeds

1 cinnamon stick (about 4 inches long)

¼ teaspoon freshly grated nutmeg

1 tablespoon pecans

2 tablespoons almonds

1 tablespoon peanuts

2 tablespoons sesame seeds

To make the paste, everything in the bowl, plus the fresh ginger, must be thoroughly blended. Working in batches, place a handful of the cooked ingredients and ginger into a blender or food processor. Set tomatoes at the bottom of each batch, and add water as needed for smoother blending. It is important to ensure that all the ingredients are completely ground.

In a large stock pot or Dutch oven, heat the remaining 3 tablespoons of the lard until it glistens and begins to smoke. Fry the mole sauce over low heat, stirring constantly for 20 minutes. During this time, incorporate the chocolate, sugar, and salt. Add the avocado leaves and fry for another 10 to 15 minutes. Keep stirring to avoid scorching. The sauce will dehydrate and turn into a paste. You'll know it's ready when a spoon dragged slowly across the bottom of the pan leaves a groove. Before using or storing the mole, remove and discard the avocado leaves. Mole paste can last for months in the refrigerator.

The mole paste can now be turned into a sauce for serving. Chicken, beef, pork, or vegetable stock are all good options for reconstituting it. You will need approximately 3 cups of stock for ½ pound of mole. It is best to use well-seasoned stock and add it ¼ cup at a time. The consistency of the finished sauce should be thick, not runny; it should generously coat the back of a spoon.

¼ cup lard or vegetable oil, divided

1 tablespoon raisins

3 seedless prunes

½ piece of pan amarillito (stale brioche or white bread will do, about the size of a dinner roll)

1 ripe plantain (to be peeled after it's cooked)

1 thin slice of fresh peeled ginger, about ¼ inch thick and 3 inches long, roughly chopped

¼ cup Oaxacan chocolate (or substitute semi-sweet chocolate plus ½ teaspoon ground cinnamon and 1 drop of almond extract)

¼ cup sugar

½ teaspoon salt

1 branch or 5 single avocado leaves, toasted

Chicken, beef, pork, or vegetable stock, as necessary

RABBIT IN OREGANO

Rabbits, oregano, and garlic are found all over the land where I grew up, so combining them came naturally. The fresh oregano really makes a difference, but dried can work as well.

———————————

Place the rabbit in a bowl, along with the lime juice and the salt. Set aside to marinate for 10 minutes.

Grind the garlic and oregano in a molcajete or mortar and pestle. Add water by the tablespoon in order to arrive at a runny paste. Add this mixture to the rabbit, making sure it fully coats the meat, and place it in the refrigerator to marinate for 30 minutes. Drain and reserve the liquid.

Heat the lard in a large cast-iron pan over medium heat. When it begins to smoke, add the rabbit and let it brown, without moving it, for approximately 8 to 10 minutes. Once the rabbit has browned, turn the pieces over and add the liquid from the marinade. Turn the heat down, cover, and let cook for 30 to 40 minutes.

Serves 4

Time: 1 hour 30 minutes

2½ pounds rabbit meat, cleaned and cut into 4-inch pieces

½ cup fresh-squeezed lime juice

½ tablespoon salt

4 cloves garlic

½ cup fresh oregano (or 2 tablespoons dried)

¼ cup lard

PUMPKIN CANDIED IN PILONCILLO

In precolonial times, calabaza tamalayota, a type of pumpkin, was cooked underground and sweetened with honey from melipona bees or syrup from the maguey (agave) plant. When the Spanish arrived, they brought honey from European bees and, later, cane sugar. These techniques allowed cooks to conserve fruits so that they could be consumed beyond the harvest season.

This is how pumpkin candied in panela—also known as calabaza en tacha—came to exist. The pumpkin was candied in the cauldrons where sugar was made. It was placed in a cylindrical basket made of palm leaves, which was then placed in the boilers where the sugar was manufactured. In the sugar mills, the concentrated cane juice was made using a combination of two boilers that were placed over a large oven called a dumbbell. One of the boilers was called "melera" and the other "tacha." The pumpkin got cooked confit style in the tacha boiler, so it was then given the name calabaza en tacha. The liquid that collected there is what we know today as piloncillo or panela. This molasses is then poured into molds where it is left until it solidifies. Ever since those times, pumpkin candied in panela has been prepared as part of the offering for the Day of the Dead.

Panela and piloncillo are the same thing; the only difference is the physical form of the solidified sugar. The name "panela" refers to the process of cooking down the cane juice to dehydrate it and solidify it in rectangular panels or in other forms.

In Oaxaca there are two types of piloncillo: one that is honey-colored and one that is dark brown. The lighter one is sweeter and more delicate in flavor, while the darker one has rustic notes of anise. Either of these can be used to make this dessert, but in order for the pumpkin to have an amber color, the lighter piloncillo must be used.

Serves 8 to 10

Time: 3 hours

1 cup lime (also known as slaked lime, calcium hydroxide, or cal)

5 quarts water, plus more as needed

6 pounds calabaza tamalayota, or pumpkin squash, in chunks

2 pounds piloncillo or panela (unrefined whole cane sugar), or substitute 3 cups dark brown sugar and ¼ cup molasses

3 cinnamon sticks

Dissolve the lime in a large pot with 5 quarts of water, enough to cover the pumpkin (it might not all dissolve). Make sure not to touch the lime with your bare hand, as it will cause burns. Submerge the pumpkin in the lime water for 20 minutes, then drain it, rinse it, and set it aside. This allows

(recipe continues)

the pumpkin to form a skin that will protect it from disintegrating when cooked in the piloncillo.

Meanwhile, bring 1 gallon of water to a boil in a large pot, along with the piloncillo (or sugar and molasses) and cinnamon. If the piloncillo is whole, you can use a knife and mallet to break it into smaller pieces. Once it boils, turn the heat down to medium and let it cook until the piloncillo (or sugar, if using) dissolves and the mixture reduces by an inch—about 1 hour.

Arrange the pumpkin pieces vertically inside the pot with the piloncillo. Cover with a lid and let boil over medium heat until the pumpkin is infused with the syrup and takes on a brownish-amber color, approximately 1 hour and 40 minutes. The pieces of pumpkin can be turned over halfway through to make sure they are evenly candied. You can also spoon the syrup over the pumpkin occasionally. It is important to ensure the pumpkin is completely cooked by the sugar and that the caramel at the bottom of the pot does not burn.

PART TWO THE COAST

arrived in Puerto Escondido, on the Oaxacan coast, on a Saturday. I was sixteen years old and had spent my savings on a bus ticket from Oaxaca city, so that night I slept on the sand. My plan was to take a three-month course on food and beverages at a technical school known as Conalep 158.

The day after my arrival, while playing soccer on the beach, I met a young man who offered me the use of a room on the roof of a building under construction, where his father was a construction worker. That was how I found my first lodgings.

That next day, I showed up at school to start studying. One afternoon as I was walking through the streets, feeling hungry and pensive, I heard a car horn honk, and turned to see a woman greeting me effusively from her car. I recognized her as a client from El Sol y la Luna, a restaurant in Oaxaca city where I had worked as a dishwasher before setting out on this adventure. The woman asked me what I was doing so far from the central valley. "Get in the car, mijo," she said. "I'm taking you to the place you're going to get a job." I obeyed and she drove us to the Hotel Santa Fe, where I ended up working for the next eight years.

At the hotel I was given a test: make a pizza for the manager. He wound up quite satisfied, not because what I served him even remotely resembled a pizza, but because I had demonstrated a talent for service, courage, and self-confidence—qualities essential for the job.

From my manager I learned hospitality and some of the rules of life by the sea, for example, that freshness takes precedence over any marinade. No snobbery here.

During this time I reached out to my brother Marco, who came to join me in Puerto Escondido a couple of years later. We found in each other the partnership necessary for success.

After years of looking after my siblings, it was on the coast that I lived my true youth. This chapter honors those years, which have profoundly influenced my cooking. I owe the refinement and precision of the seafood, shellfish, cocktails, and ceviches at Casa Oaxaca to the fishermen who taught me the essentials of these ingredients, and to the women who waited on the beach to bring the day's catch to their kitchens.

Food there is cooked with the same rigor as in the central valley or on the Isthmus, a region of Mexico that is home to one of the country's largest indigenous populations, but with a different character. The object is to feel happy, and to seek the same for those around you, with a very cold beer and a bowl of salt to toss on the shrimp cocktail: life is to be enjoyed. Work seems a lot like pleasure, and fresh, simple cooking invites people to come together.

Puerto Escondido was a time of my life full of meaningful discoveries, sometimes deciphered in the kitchen, sometimes in life itself, but always in complementary ways, almost always taken from the same point of reference: the ocean as a milpa, as a mother, as a wild gesture of life.

VUELVE A LA VIDA

Vuelve a la vida is a generic name for a dish that can be found in the culinary lexicon of every Pacific region. It can be made with octopus, scallops, shrimp, conch, fish, all of these together or a combination of whatever is on hand.

————————————

Mix the onion, tomato, cilantro, shrimp, octopus, conch meat, and salt in a bowl. Serve in individual bowls, and garnish with the avocado.

Serve alongside hot sauces, saltine crackers, and lime wedges so that diners may season to their liking.

Serves 4

Time: 20 minutes (if the shellfish is precooked)

¼ cup onion, finely chopped

¼ cup tomato, seeded and finely chopped

¼ cup cilantro, finely chopped

3½ ounces small shrimp, cooked

3½ ounces octopus, cooked and cut into ½-inch cubes

3½ ounces conch meat, cooked and cut into ½-inch cubes

1 tablespoon salt

To serve

1 avocado, sliced

Hot sauces (Tabasco, Valentina, Cholula, or Búfalo brands)

Saltine crackers

4 limes, cut into wedges

PESCADILLAS

When this recipe is made in Puerto Escondido the fish used is barrilete or skipjack, which belongs to the tuna family. The wood over which it is smoked deepens the fish's flavors, giving it an extraordinary taste. It is also common to fill pescadillas using pescado de baja, or the cheapest fish at the market.

If skipjack tuna is not available, a firm, white-fleshed fish will work as well, but tuna varieties will give it a deeper flavor which will best resemble barrilete.

To make the tuna, preheat a pan or grill for at least 5 minutes. Pat dry the tuna steak and coat with oil. Once the grill is hot, season the tuna steak generously with salt and pepper. Cook until it's well seared, about 2 to 3 minutes on each side, or until fully cooked. You want it to be well done so that it will flake easily and absorb all the juices from the tomato sofrito. Remove from the grill, let it cool slightly, flake with a fork, and set aside.

To make the sofrito, heat the olive oil in a large sauté pan. Add the onions, garlic, and a pinch of salt, and cook stirring often until golden and starting to brown on the edges.

Add the tomato and cook for 2 more minutes. Then add the olives, capers, and reserved fish and leave to cook for about 5 minutes. Finally, incorporate the cilantro, cover, and let cook for another 5 minutes, until the flavors are melded. Season with salt to taste and set aside.

To make the salsa, in an ungreased skillet over medium heat, roast the chiles, stirring constantly until their color deepens and they release a toasty aroma, about 2 minutes. Remove the pan from the heat, and pour in ½ cup of water to soften the chiles. Transfer chiles along with their water to a blender, and purée with the garlic and the salt. Add more water as needed. The salsa should be thick and smooth. Strain and set aside.

To make the guacamole, coarsely mash the avocados, then add the onion, cilantro, and salt, and mix well.

To make the pescadillas, heat the vegetable oil in a heavy pan or cast-iron skillet. Meanwhile, if the tortillas are not freshly made, warm them

(recipe continues)

Serves 4

Time: 45 minutes

For the grilled tuna

1 1-pound fresh tuna steak or any firm, white-fleshed fish

Vegetable or canola oil

Salt

Freshly ground black pepper

For the tomato sofrito

¼ cup olive oil

¼ cup onion, diced

2 cloves garlic, minced

Salt, to taste

1½ cups tomato, diced

6 green olives, minced

1½ tablespoons capers, roughly chopped

½ cup chopped cilantro

For the salsa

3 chiles guajillos, stemmed

½ cup water, plus more as needed

1 clove garlic

1 teaspoon salt

For the guacamole

2 avocados

2 tablespoons onion, diced

2 tablespoons chopped cilantro (including the stem)

1 tablespoon salt

up by wrapping them in a dish towel and microwaving them for a couple of seconds. This will soften them and prevent them from breaking when assembling the pescadillas. Place two tablespoons of the fish filling in each tortilla and fold in half. (Weaving a toothpick through the edge of the tortilla will help keep the filling inside when frying.)

Gently place a few pescadillas at a time in the hot oil. Dip a corner in first and make sure bubbles form around it as it touches the oil. This indicates that the temperature is ideal. Fry until golden brown, turning over as necessary. Remove and place on paper towels to drain off the excess oil.

Serve while still warm, along with the salsa, guacamole, and lime wedges.

For the pescadillas
1 cup vegetable oil, for frying
12 corn tortillas
Lime wedges, for serving

THE BEST OF THE OAXACAN OCEANS

On the coasts of Oaxaca we find red snapper, sea bream, mahi-mahi, sea bass, sailfish, horse mackerel, bonito tuna, jack fish, and mullet. Fishermen from this region have always caught these marvels using traditional methods—fishing with lines and harpoons—for their own consumption and to be sold commercially at local and regional markets.

I know many fishermen from Puerto Escondido, but in recent years I have established a professional relationship with Eduardo Hernández. A native Oaxacan like me, he did not learn his trade on the coasts of our state, but rather in Baja California, where Eduardo worked for many years fishing and exporting fish and shellfish to Japan and Korea.

Due to the demands of these clients, Eduardo and his brother Ezequiel learned Japanese techniques of fish management more than thirty years ago. Ike jime, which translates literally as "fishing by the minute," means that once a fish is caught—gently and without striking it, to avoid any unnecessary stress—it must be cut very precisely, bled out, cleaned, and put on crushed ice. This method demonstrates respect for the life of the fish and for the fish as a product, guaranteeing freshness and preserving the original flavor.

Operating in this way, the Hernández brothers began to market seafood within Mexico. Ezequiel stayed in Baja California, Eduardo returned to Oaxaca. Together they have become the primary seafood vendors for Casa Oaxaca as well as many of the most successful restaurants in Mexico.

To this day, whenever I travel to Puerto Escondido, I board a boat with Eduardo and we go fishing.

TIRITAS DE PESCADO

In a nonreactive bowl, toss fish with lime juice, olive oil, oregano, and salt. Marinate for 10 minutes. Add the cucumber and the onion and refrigerate for another 5 minutes. Add salt to taste and serve with tortilla chips.

Serves 4

Time: 30 minutes

7 ounces fresh, skinless white fish (preferably sierra or mahi-mahi) cut into 2-inch-long strips (¼ inch thick)

½ cup fresh lime juice

1 tablespoon olive oil

½ teaspoon dried oregano

½ tablespoon salt, plus more to taste

½ cup thinly sliced cucumber, peeled and deseeded

½ cup red onion, julienned

Salt to taste

Tortilla chips, for serving

MARGARITA SCALLOP COCKTAIL

When making ceviches that are not refrigerated, it is important to mix the ingredients in a bowl set in an ice bath. This way, the ceviche will be at the optimal temperature when served.

Serves 4
Time: 45 minutes

1 cup fresh lime juice

¼ cup olive oil

1 tablespoon salt

½ cup red onion, julienned

1 teaspoon chile chiltepín, toasted and finely ground

2 cups cucumber, peeled and deseeded, sliced into half circles

14 ounces scallops, cut into small cubes

½ cup peanuts, roasted and peeled

1 sliced avocado, to garnish

Saltine crackers, for serving

Cilantro flowers to garnish

Fill a large bowl with ice and a bit of water. Place a smaller bowl inside, where you'll prepare the ceviche. Add the lime juice, olive oil, and salt, and stir until the salt dissolves.

Add the red onion, chile chiltepín, and cucumber and set aside for 5 minutes. Add the scallops and leave to marinate for 15 minutes, stirring occasionally. Divide into bowls, garnish with peanuts and avocado, and serve with saltine crackers and garnished with cilantro flowers.

DEEP FRIED WHOLE FISH

Fried fish is served all around the globe, whether it is prepared whole, in filets, or in pieces. This is the simple, most immediate and delicious food of fishermen the world over. It's a popular street food in Portugal and Spain, where it shows up marinated in adobo, fried and sold in paper cones, or as delicate fresh anchovies tart with vinegar and lightly dredged in flour before frying. It is also a typical dish around Asia's coasts, where its preparation is uncannily similar to Mexico's: juicy inside, crunchy outside. No particular fish is specified in this recipe, as I always say the freshest fish is best, but snapper or sea bass are good options. Always make sure the oil is very hot before frying, otherwise you'll end up with exceedingly oily fish.

―――――――――――

To make the salsa verde, place the miltomates or tomatillos, with the jalapeños, onion, cilantro, lime juice, and salt in a blender, process until smooth, and set aside.

To make the fish, place garlic, lime juice, salt, and pepper in a blender and process until well incorporated. Using a sharp knife make 3 or 4 diagonal cuts along the body of each fish, cutting until the knife meets the bone. Do this on both sides of each fish. Coat the fish with the garlic-lime mixture and let marinate for 20 minutes.

Heat the vegetable oil in a large cast-iron skillet over high heat.

Place the flour in a shallow dish and lightly dredge the fish all over, shaking off any excess. This will ensure a crispier texture and keep the fish from sticking to the pan. Test the oil by frying a piece of tortilla. When bubbles surround the tortilla and the oil is shimmering, it's ready. Carefully lower a fish into the skillet head first. Fry the fish one by one, until the flesh is cooked and they turn a crispy golden brown, about 8 to 10 minutes per side. Be careful to turn them over away from you, and do it gently so as to not spill oil onto the flame. Place on a wire rack to drain briefly.

To make the salad, place the onion, avocado, and tomatoes on a plate and season with lime juice and salt.

Serve with salsa verde, tortillas, and lime wedges.

Serves 4

Time: 45 minutes

For the salsa verde

6 miltomates or tomatillos, boiled in water for 8 to 10 minutes or until they soften and turn yellowish green

2 jalapeños

2 tablespoons onion, diced

1 tablespoon chopped cilantro

2 tablespoons fresh lime juice

½ teaspoon salt

For the fish

6 garlic cloves

½ cup fresh lime juice

1 tablespoon salt

¼ teaspoon ground black pepper

4 1-pound fish, gutted and cleaned

4 cups vegetable oil

1 cup flour

For the salad

½ onion, sliced into wedges

1 avocado, cut into wedges

2 tomatoes, cut into wedges

2 tablespoons fresh lime juice

1 teaspoon salt

To serve

Warm tortillas (approximately 1 pound)

4 limes, cut into wedges

PICADO, FLAG OF THE ISTHMUS

Lleve totopo mamá,
camarón seco,
tamalito de iguana,
compre mamá.

The market of Juchitán, a town in the southeast of Oaxaca state, is one of the most fascinating places of its kind, full of color and heat, diaphanous skirts that sweep the floors, shining faces framed by earrings of yellow gold. In corridor after corridor you find fish, green mangoes, cheese, and many other local ingredients, as well as embroidery and jewelry with which to adorn yourself.

You might hear a Zapotec melody, mixed with Spanish. The Isthmus is a region in the states of Oaxaca and Veracruz that contains one of the largest indigenous populations in the country. It is situated between the Gulf of Mexico and the Pacific Ocean. Prior to the Panama Canal, it was a major shipping route and it has swampy dense jungles that house the majority of terrestrial biodiversity in the country, but also thick pine forests where the Oaxacan Sierra Madre flattens to a plateau. Ethnic groups like the Huaves, Zapotecos, and Zoques peacefully coexist in the Isthmus, and it is a land of verses and velvety songs, hands that paint and embroider flowers, fishermen, salespeople, and the coming together of diverse elements of Mexican culture. Hammocks rock the dreams of a thousand children under the tamarind trees, while a singular cuisine is cooked over the slow flames of the fogones.

The Isthmus's distinctive culture is the result of the most exotic mixing of identities: its population is Zapote, Huave, Mixe, Zoque, Lebanese, Iraqi, Spanish, and Chinese, to mention just a few of those who live side by side. The festive and traditional flower-painted jicapextles, vessels whose interiors proffer a variety of fruits stuck with small flags of finely cut papel picado, are a metaphor for the community as a whole.

Here they say that when man landed on the moon there was already a woman from Juchitán selling totopos, or tortilla chips. This demonstrates the importance of two things in this region: commerce and the reach of its gastronomy.

Both go back to the exchanges that enriched the East as well as New Spain. The ancient shawls from Manila and the beautiful wardrobes worn by Istmeña women have common roots. Something similar happens with food: dishes from the Isthmus prepared to celebrate a vela, the most important celebration of the Isthmus of Tehuantepec, are delicately flavored with spices from other worlds.

Living side by side, all the different cultures remake themselves in a shared space, shaped to a singularly integrated society—that of the Isthmus. Towns that were established with the arrival of the railroad and European migration today delight in roasted iguana and plums recently plucked from the trees.

PRAWNS WITH MOJO DE AJO

Using the flat part of a knife, crush the garlic and then roughly chop it. In a large bowl, mix the chopped garlic, lime juice, salt, and ⅓ cup water.

Place the prawns in the bowl and marinate them in the garlic mixture for at least 15 minutes.

Melt the butter in a large pan. Once it bubbles, add the marinade with the prawns. Depending on the size of your pan, this might have to be done in batches. Make sure that the prawns stay in contact with the pan as much as possible. When they turn red and begin to brown, turn them over and keep frying until they achieve the same color on both sides, about 5 minutes per batch. Make sure the garlic browns without turning black, as that will make the flavor bitter. Serve warm.

Serves 4
Time: 30 minutes

16 cloves garlic, peeled
4 tablespoons fresh
  lime juice
1 tablespoon salt
⅓ cup water
12 prawns, cleaned,
  shells on
1 stick unsalted butter

CHILATE

Chilate is a beverage whose ingredients vary according to the customs of each region. On the coast of Oaxaca it is made with cacao and rice, while in Guerrero, the state to the north, it is prepared with corn. Some people add anise, ginger, or pepper, and there are even those who substitute piloncillo—unrefined cane sugar—for the sugar.

Serves 4

Time: 12 hours to soak and 45 minutes to cook

Water, as needed

½ cup white long-grain rice

½ cup whole cacao beans

2 cinnamon sticks

½ cup sugar

1 cup evaporated milk

Wash the rice and place in a bowl. Cover with water and leave to soak overnight.

Toast the cacao on a comal or in a cast-iron skillet over low heat, stirring often for 20 to 25 minutes, or until the whole room smells of chocolate. The beans will change color, and disintegrate when bitten. Set aside to cool. Peel by taking each bean in your hand, pressing it, and rubbing the cacao to loosen its outer skin. If it's well roasted, the skin will come off easily.

Strain the soaked rice, and place in a blender along with the cacao, cinnamon sticks, sugar, and evaporated milk. Process until everything is finely ground. Strain through a cheesecloth or fine mesh sieve, discarding the solids, and add enough water to end up with 4 cups total. Serve with ice.

MANGOS SWEETENED IN CHILE DE ÁRBOL

Mix the lime with 4 cups of water. Stir until mostly dissolved (it may not all dissolve). Make sure not to touch the lime with your bare hand as it can cause burns.

Submerge the mangoes in the lime water and soak for 20 minutes. Drain and rinse.

Place the mangos in a small pot and add enough water to cover. Add the sugar, chiles, and all of the spices and bring to a boil. Once the water reaches a rolling boil, lower the heat until the liquid begins to bubble and thicken, then let cook at a steady boil for 30 to 40 minutes. When finished, the syrup should have a consistency a bit thinner than honey.

Let cool and slice before serving.

Serves 4

Time: 1 hour

¼ cup lime (also known as slaked lime, calcium hydroxide, or cal)

4 cups water

4 firm mangos (with partially green skin), peeled

½ cup sugar

2 chiles de árbol

2 cloves

1 cinnamon stick

2 allspice berries

PART THREE CASA OAXACA

Casa Oaxaca is an expression of many Oaxacan traditions, starting with the most popular: hospitality. The whole idea behind the small group of restaurants that bear the Casa Oaxaca name is to open the doors of Oaxaca to travelers and diners who seek to explore its origins.

Casa Oaxaca is a hearth where what is remote and mysterious about Oaxaca's traditional foods becomes familiar and accessible. Here you can try the distinctive moles that are prepared in the different regions according to the celebration at hand and the season of the year, with the peace of mind that we are respecting their foundational elements, even though we might have tweaked them for seasoned diners.

Corn, an essential ingredient in Oaxacan cooking, one that can be found in every meal, is widely represented in memelas, tostadas for appetizers, warm tortillas, tacos, tejate, and in sopa de guías (page 35).

The distinctive functions and flavors of wild herbs can be experienced in chepil tamales (page 45) and in sopa de frijolón (page 120) and rabbit in oregano (page 61). Chiles, both fresh and dried, are served in salsas, ceviches, and more labor-intensive dishes such as moles. Dishes from the Isthmus and the coast are prepared, as well as recipes from the Chinantla region and also the Sierra Mixe to the east. We use ancient techniques and traditional instruments to reinterpret Oaxacan food for today's world.

Mezcal is an important part of our menu. As the popular saying goes, "El mezcal es el camino"—mezcal is the way. Casa Oaxaca offers a carefully chosen variety of artisanal mezcals from different maestros mezcaleros (master mezcal makers) that use different species of agave and different processes of distillation, like espadín, arroqueño, madrecuixe, barril, and tobalá mezcals; produced in Matatlán or in Santa Catarina Minas, in San Bartolo or in San Juan; in copper, in leather, or in clay. Mezcals from every region and every tradition. We serve mezcals with notes of herbs or of smoke, of mesquite or of red earth. Soft mezcals and strong mezcals, to drink to remember and to drink to forget.

The restaurant occupies a colonial building, filled with locally made objects: red-clay plates, molcajetes used to prepare salsas tableside, embroidered clothes for the staff, and decidedly Oaxacan vegetation nestled around the dining room. Casa Oaxaca is a place for those who seek not generic luxury, but rather the greatest luxury of all: the feeling of being immersed in local culture.

SALSA DE MOLCAJETE

At Casa Oaxaca, this fresh salsa is offered to each table. Diners are asked if they'd like it green or red, spicy or mild.

Serves 4

Time: 20 minutes

Roast the chiles in a preheated, ungreased skillet or pan over medium heat for about 3 minutes, or until they change color and parts of their skin are blackened. Then roast either the tomatoes or miltomates, depending on which you are using, until parts of their skin are charred and they are soft to the touch.

Grind the garlic and salt in a molcajete with the tejolote (or with a mortar and pestle). Once it makes a paste, add the chiles and grind again. When the ingredients are completely crushed, add the tomatoes or miltomates and grind once more. You want the salsa to be chunky.

Stir in the onion and cilantro. Taste for salt, and if you prefer a more liquid consistency, add a drizzle of water.

This salsa is for general use and can be served with ceviche tostadas, quesadillas, or any other dish you feel like.

3 jalapeño chiles

7 ounces jitomate guajillo or Roma tomatoes (for red salsa), or 7 ounces miltomates (or tomatillos), outer leaves removed (for green)

1 clove garlic

½ tablespoon salt

1 tablespoon diced onion

1 tablespoon chopped fresh cilantro, stem included

CHAMOY CEVICHE

To make the chamoy, place the hibiscus flowers along with 3 cups of water in a saucepan, and boil for 10 to 15 minutes. With a slotted spoon, remove and discard the flowers. Add the tamarind, passion fruit, lime and orange juices, sugar, and worm salt to the hibiscus infusion. Boil over medium heat until the liquid has reduced by half. Stir occasionally to make sure it doesn't burn. The chamoy will become thick and syrupy; it is done when it coats the back of a spoon and leaves a visible mark when you drag your finger across it. This can take around 2 hours. When the chamoy is at the desired consistency, strain, cool, and reserve.

To make the ceviche, mix the lime juice, salt, olive oil, and oregano and stir until the salt dissolves. Add the cubed fish and refrigerate for at least 30 minutes.

To serve, cut the fruits into ½-inch cubes and set them aside. Take the fish out of the refrigerator. The flesh should have turned from translucent to opaque and will feel firm to the touch. Using a slotted spoon, place the fish cubes onto a paper towel to remove any excess juice. Place 5 or 6 pieces of fish on each plate, and divide the cubed fruit evenly among them. Arrange the radish slices, avocado cones, spring onion rings, cherry tomato halves, serrano slices, and cilantro flowers over the fish and fruit. Serve the chamoy tableside, pouring it around the fish and fruit until it just covers the bottom of the dish.

Serves 4
Time: 3 hours

For the chamoy

1 cup dried hibiscus flowers
3 cups water
3 tablespoons tamarind pulp
3 tablespoons passion fruit pulp
½ cup fresh lime juice
1 cup fresh orange juice
½ cup sugar
2 tablespoons sal de gusano (worm salt)

For the ceviche

½ cup fresh lime juice
½ teaspoon salt
¼ cup olive oil
1 teaspoon dried oregano
3 ounces fresh, skinless white fish, such as grouper or bass, cut into ¾-inch cubes

To serve

2 slices pineapple
1 mango
2 slices watermelon
2 radishes, thinly sliced into rounds
¼ avocado, cut into thin slices and rolled into cones
1 spring onion, sliced into rings
12 cherry tomatoes, each cut in half
1 serrano chile, thinly sliced into rounds
1 bunch cilantro flowers for garnish

HOJA SANTA ROLLS

If you have the bean paste ready, this appetizer is easy to make. Rolling the hoja santa, an aromatic herb that is ubiquitous in Mexican cooking for its unique taste, to form the tacos or taquitos takes practice, but once you get the hang of it, it goes quickly. Hoja santa should be handled with care as it is delicate. The size of the leaf determines the serving, so if a leaf is quite small you may use two, letting one overlap the other. Likewise, if the leaf has holes, you can place a smaller leaf over it to keep the filling from spilling out.

———————————

Blanch the hoja santa leaves in boiling water, then soak them in an ice bath. Remove and gently pat dry with a dish towel.

Place a leaf on a cutting board with the bottom side of the leaf (where its veins feel most pronounced) facing up. Using a sharp knife, make a cut along each side of the widest vertical vein and another small cut on the upper side to remove the stem (which is too tough to eat). Repeat for the remaining hoja santa leaves. Set them aside.

To make the chapulines, preheat a pan over a medium-high heat. Sauté the chapulines in the vegetable oil along with the garlic and lime juice. Cook for a couple of minutes or until the chapulines are brown and crisp. Set aside.

To make the salsa, place the chile guajillo into a bowl and pour the boiling water over it to soften. Once the chile guajillo is soft, place it along with the water into a blender with the garlic and the salt and purée until smooth. Set aside.

Place an hoja santa leaf on a flat surface, with the softer, brighter side facing down and the narrow tip toward the top. Take about 1 tablespoon of bean paste and spread it horizontally, off-center and more toward the lower part of the leaf. Leave a space of about 2 inches clear of bean paste on the left, right, and bottom edges of the leaf. Sprinkle the string cheese and chapulines on top of the bean paste.

To form a small taco, or taquito, take the vertical edges of the leaf and fold them toward the middle. Then take the bottom edge, the one closest to you, and fold it up. Now roll from bottom to top, making as compact

(recipe continues)

Serves 4

Time: 45 minutes

For the hoja santa rolls

12 hoja santa leaves

½ cup bean paste (page 40)

½ cup Oaxacan string cheese, shredded and roughly chopped

1 tablespoon vegetable oil, for sautéing

For the chapulines

½ cup chapulines

2 tablespoons vegetable oil

1 clove garlic, chopped

1 teaspoon fresh lime juice

For the guajillo salsa

1 chile guajillo, deveined and seeds removed

½ cup boiling hot water

½ clove garlic

1 teaspoon salt

To serve

¼ cup crema

¼ cup crumbled queso fresco (or feta cheese)

1 radish, sliced (for garnish)

1 tablespoon red onion, thinly sliced (for garnish)

Cilantro, sprouts or leaves (for garnish)

a roll as possible as you do this. Set aside and repeat with the remaining hoja santa leaves.

Add a tablespoon of oil to a pan over medium-low heat. Take an hoja santa roll and place it into the pan. It helps to place the rolled side down; this way it seals the taco and prevents it from coming apart. Cook for about 1 minute, turning the roll over, until it's golden brown. Avoid over-cooking, as it will turn the leaf bitter and brittle. Repeat for the remaining rolls.

To serve, even out the tacos by trimming their ends with a sharp knife, then cut the tacos into two or three sections, depending on the size of the leaf. Pour some guajillo salsa onto each plate, and place the taquitos on top. Garnish with crema, cheese, radish, red onion, and cilantro.

IN THE BEGINNING THERE
WAS THE MERCADO DE ABASTOS

Casa Oaxaca and the food we serve is intimately linked to our purveyors, the men and women who get ingredients to the kitchen in their best condition. The Mercado de Abastos is one of my main resources for obtaining herbs, grains, chiles, vegetables, and fruit.

At least once a week—but sometimes up to four times weekly—one (or all) of the kitchen managers and I go in search of tomates riñón and chiles de agua, hibiscus flowers, jicamas and chapulines, miltomates and hierba de conejo, chiles de pasilla, and garlic, pineapple, and fresh coconut.

Sometimes I also bring journalists, travelers, and tourists who want to know more, or even friends and colleagues. While I primarily go to the Abastos market to buy for the restaurant, it's also an excursion. There is always a snack along the way: when there's time, a memela from La Güera (page 189) or a taco de barbacoa enchilada from Tlacolula (page 197)—when there's not, some fruit or a little Oaxacan string cheese.

This market is not distinguished by its beauty, but rather the quality, value, and abundance of its offerings: if something is Oaxacan, you'll find it at the Abastos. It's safe to say the landscape of this market is seen nowhere else. Musicians stroll by with their instruments, the vendors, wearing traditional regional clothing, carry enormous baskets on their heads. A woman sits on the floor making Oaxacan string cheese, there are children running along the smoky corridors, and men pushing dollies loaded with ingredients that come from every corner of the state. People pass by carrying clay comales; there are stands with all kinds of petates, metates, molcajetes, pots, and metal grills. You see large bundles of lime, heirloom beans, baskets, buckets, and huacales (crates) coming in from the milpas, bursting with corn, quelites, and all the other produce from this land.

JÍCAMA TACOS

These "tacos" are actually made with jícama slices instead of tortillas. The jícama must be cut paper-thin so that it can be rolled. A trick we use at the restaurant, when the jícama is tough, is to cut it and then coat the slices with melted butter, place them on a sheet pan, and bake them for 5 minutes or until softened. Jícama is in season from September through May, during which time it is at its juiciest and sweetest.

To make the tacos, place the jícama slices in a bowl filled with ice water and set aside. Before using, pat them dry with a clean dish cloth.

Meanwhile, to make the salsa, purée all the ingredients in a blender and set aside.

To make the guacamole, blend all the ingredients and the ¼ cup water in a blender and set aside.

To make the huitlacoche, heat the oil in a pan and add the onion, garlic, huitlacoche, epazote, and salt. Cook for about 5 minutes. Set aside.

To assemble the tacos, take two jícama slices and place one over the other so that their edges overlap, forming a longer, oblong shape. Make a horizontal line of filling using: 1 tablespoon huitlacoche, 1 tablespoon chapulines, and 1 tablespoon of string cheese. The filling should be placed off-center, toward the lower third of the jícama.

Roll up the tacos starting from the edge closest to you. In batches of no more than three, brown the tacos in a pan with a little butter. Seal each taco by placing the side of the taco with the end of the jícama slice in first; this will prevent it from unraveling as you turn to cook it. Let it brown for about 2 minutes without

(recipe continues)

Serves 4
Time: 45 minutes

For the tacos

30 very thin slices of jícama (from a whole jícama that is more oval than round in shape, peeled and cut with a mandoline or knife)

½ cup chapulines

1 cup Oaxacan string cheese, shredded and chopped

2 tablespoons unsalted butter

For the salsa

6 miltomates or tomatillos, boiled in water for 8 to 10 minutes or until they soften and turn yellowish green

2 tablespoons onion, roughly chopped

1 tablespoon cilantro, roughly chopped, stem included

2 tablespoons fresh lime juice

½ teaspoon salt

For the guacamole

1 avocado

1 tablespoon onion, roughly chopped

½ tablespoon cilantro, roughly chopped, stem included

1 tablespoon fresh lime juice

½ teaspoon salt

¼ cup water

moving it, then turn it over and repeat so that it browns on all sides. Repeat for the remaining tacos.

To serve, pour some salsa onto the middle of each plate and place three tacos on top. Garnish with guacamole, queso fresco (or feta), tortilla strips, cherry tomatoes, radish slices, and cilantro sprouts.

For the huitlacoche

2 tablespoons vegetable oil

¼ cup diced onion

2 cloves garlic, minced

1½ cups huitlacoche

4 epazote leaves, sliced (or dried, if fresh is not available)

Pinch of salt

To serve

¼ cup queso fresco (or feta cheese), crumbled (for garnish)

2 corn tortillas, julienned and fried (for garnish)

20 cherry tomatoes (for garnish)

10 radish slices (for garnish)

Cilantro sprouts (for garnish)

DUCK GARNACHAS

At first glance, guacachile might look like guacamole, but its preparation is closer to that of mayonnaise. To prevent separation, pay close attention to the temperature of the ingredients, as well as the way they are mixed.

Following the recipe on page 14, use the masa to make small tortillas 3 inches in diameter and ⅛ inch thick. As you take each tortilla off the griddle or comal, and while they are still hot, pinch the edges. This rim will help contain the duck carnitas as you baste and fry the garnacha with oil.

Mix the duck meat with the onion. Scoop some mixture onto the rimmed tortilla, and press it down so that there is a tightly packed mound on each. Cover and place them in the refrigerator for about 30 minutes.

Meanwhile, to make the guacachile, heat a tablespoon of olive oil in a pan and sauté the garlic and onion. Once the edges begin to burn, add the serrano chiles and cook for about 2 more minutes. You don't want to burn the chiles, just look for when they turn bright green, and then remove and set the mixture aside to cool. It's very important to let everything come to room temperature before continuing, as this will keep the guacachile from separating. Once cooled, put the garlic-onion-chile mixture into a blender along with the salt. Add the remaining olive oil in a thin, constant drizzle so that the mixture emulsifies. Set aside.

To make the pickled cabbage, place the vinegar, hibiscus flowers, and salt into a small pan. Heat until bubbles begin to form around the edges. Pour the vinegar mix over the shredded cabbage and marinate for about 30 minutes or until the cabbage takes on a fuchsia color. Drain and set aside.

Just before serving, heat ½ cup of oil in a pan. Tilt the pan to form a pool of oil, taking care not to spill it. Put three of the garnachas in the upper part of the pan, tortilla side down, and use a spoon to bathe them with the hot oil. The duck and the tortilla should turn golden brown and crisp. Repeat for the remaining garnachas, frying each batch of three in another ½ cup of oil. Make sure to heat the oil before starting the next batch.

Serve three garnachas on each plate, and garnish with a teaspoon of guacachile, some cabbage, a sprinkle of queso fresco (or feta), and herb sprouts or leaves for color.

Serves 4

Time: 1 hour

For the garnachas

2 pounds masa (page 8)

½ recipe of duck for garnachas (page 143)

2 tablespoons onion, finely diced

2 cups vegetable oil

For the guacachile

⅓ cup olive oil (1 tablespoon to sauté the garlic and onion, the rest to emulsify the guacachile)

1 clove garlic

⅓ onion, chopped

4 serrano chiles

1 teaspoon salt

For the pickled cabbage

¼ cup white vinegar

¼ cup dried hibiscus flowers

1 teaspoon salt

½ cup red cabbage, shredded

To serve

Crumbled queso fresco (or feta cheese)

Sprouts or leaves of any kind of herb (nasturtium, cilantro, or radish sprouts are ideal)

CEVICHE VERDE WITH MAHI-MAHI

This is an unusual ceviche, made with juicy, sweet, lightly acidic fruits. Since everything is covered with a creamy avocado dressing, diners have trouble deciphering exactly what's in the ceviche—they simply give themselves over to enjoying it.

———————————

To prepare the ceviche, cut all the fish, fruits, and vegetables into ½-inch dice. Mix the mahi-mahi, lime juice, olive oil, oregano, and salt in a glass or stainless-steel bowl. Cover, and refrigerate for about 1 hour. Make sure that everything is completely submerged in the liquid.

Drain and add the cucumber, pear, pineapple, miltomates, plums, grapes, avocado, coconut, and cilantro and set aside.

To make the dressing, combine the miltomates, avocado, cilantro, and salt, plus ¼ cup of water in a blender, and process until smooth. Add to the bowl with the fish and fruit and mix until evenly incorporated.

To serve, divide the mixture among four plates, and garnish with slices of fresh coconut, pomegranate seeds, and cilantro sprouts. Serve alongside tortilla chips as desired.

Serves 4

Time: 1 hour 20 minutes

For the ceviche

1 pound fresh, skinless mahi-mahi

1 cup fresh lime juice

¼ cup olive oil

1 teaspoon oregano

1 tablespoon salt

¼ cup cucumber, peeled, seeded

¼ cup pear, peeled

¼ cup pineapple

¼ cup miltomates or tomatillos

¼ cup plums

¼ cup green seedless grapes

¼ cup avocado

½ cup fresh, young coconut meat

¼ cup cilantro, chopped

For the dressing

3 tomatillos

½ avocado

¼ cup cilantro, roughly chopped

1 teaspoon salt

¼ cup water

To garnish

¼ cup fresh coconut, thinly sliced

¼ cup pomegranate seeds

Cilantro sprouts (optional)

Tortilla chips (optional)

MY GARDEN

Quality control for ingredients has been the central concern of chefs around the world for the past ten to fifteen years to such a degree that some even build their own gardens to stock their restaurants.

Growing up in the countryside, I learned about agriculture long before I found my calling as a chef.

My garden—which supplies 70 percent of the produce for two of my restaurants—grows in the midst of the arid landscape of La Raya de Zimatlán, on a plot of land that has belonged to my family for many years. It is run by my uncle Sergio, and is home to kohlrabi, radishes, tomatoes, miltomates, hoja santa, plantains, all the herbs imaginable, broccoli, carrots, and lettuce. There is a compost zone that eventually fertilizes the planted land and we raise rabbits, and fish for trout in a tank whose water also irrigates the land. There is a goat for milking, and mayordomías, or parties, are organized at the garden. Sometimes the whole family gathers to eat a meal, and on these occasions I bring my friends, or student chefs, or guests and diners from the hotel, to spend the afternoon and cook with the bounty of the land. I involve my family as well as my work team in the project; it is on this plot that my professional and personal lives come together.

My garden has a dual significance: on one hand it is an extension of my family's traditional milpa, and on the other it is a site for experimenting with new crops.

REQUESÓN- (OR RICOTTA-) STUFFED SQUASH BLOSSOMS

This recipe is similar to the Italian dish Fiori di Zucca Ripieni di Ricotta. But instead of using basil and lemon juice for acid, at Casa Oaxaca I incorporate the sweet touch of honey and the very Mexican note of herbaceous epazote.

Serves 4
Time: 45 minutes

To make the sweet potato chips, heat the vegetable oil to about 355–365°F in a deep skillet or fryer. To test the heat, drop a grain of rice into the oil—it should rise to the surface and begin to fry instantly.

While the oil heats up, peel and cut off the tips of the sweet potatoes. With a knife or mandoline, cut them lengthwise into 1⁄16-inch-thick slices. Place them in ice-cold water and soak for about 10 minutes.

Remove the sweet potatoes from the water and pat them dry with a dish cloth.

Fry the slices in 1-layer batches until they turn golden brown, about 1 to 2 minutes. If they curl, the oil is too hot and the temperature should be lowered. Remove and drain on a paper towel. Dust with salt while they're hot. Set them aside and reserve the oil, allowing it to cool, to use the next time you are frying.

To make the epazote oil, heat 1⁄2 cup of olive oil in a small skillet over medium heat. Fry the epazote leaves 5 at a time for 2 to 3 seconds, until crisp. Drain the leaves on paper towels and set the oil aside to cool. Once leaves and oil have cooled, place them in a blender and process with a teaspoon of salt and the reserved room-temperature oil, adding the oil in a thin, constant drizzle. Strain through a fine colander covered with cheesecloth and reserve.

To make the squash blossoms, heat 1 tablespoon olive oil in a pan and sauté the onion and garlic until translucent. Add the ricotta, honey, chopped epazote, salt, and pepper. Cook for 2 minutes, stirring constantly. Set aside to cool slightly.

When ready to serve, take the ricotta mixture and carefully fill the squash blossoms. In a skillet, heat a drizzle of olive oil, and cook the filled blossoms for about 2 minutes, turning them over gently. To serve, place a squash blossom on a sweet potato chip, drizzle with a few drops of epazote oil, and sprinkle with crushed pumpkin seeds.

For the sweet potato chips

1½ cups vegetable oil
2 sweet potatoes
½ teaspoon salt

For the epazote oil

½ cup olive oil
15 fresh epazote leaves
1 teaspoon salt

For the squash blossoms

1 tablespoon olive oil plus more for cooking the blossoms
2 tablespoons onion, finely chopped
¼ clove garlic, finely chopped
1 cup ricotta
2 tablespoons honey
1 tablespoon fresh epazote, finely chopped (or dried, if fresh is not available)
Pinch of salt
Pinch of pepper
12 flores de calabaza (squash blossoms)

To serve

2 tablespoons pumpkin seeds, toasted and gently crushed with a mortar and pestle

SOPA DE FRIJOLÓN

The frijolón is also known as ayocote, which means "large bean." It's an heirloom bean, kidney-shaped and about the size of a fava bean. Its color is a grayish purple and it is normally flecked with black. Acquiring frijolones requires a meticulous search, and the same goes for their blossoms. Finding them also depends on the season.

This recipe is simple in its essence; however, the beans' starches can be unpredictable. While the recipe calls for 1½ cups of broth for the soup, it's necessary to understand the desired texture and adjust the liquid appropriately for each batch. If the frijolón was not recently harvested (to check this, it's wise to ask the vendor) increase the soaking time, starting the afternoon before the soup is to be prepared. If you can't find frijolón, you can use black beans, or perhaps another kind of bean, but always remember the aforementioned rule. One of the telltale signs that the soup is well made is a pale green halo that forms at the edges of the soup once it's served.

The bean's flower (which is a vermilion color) is used here as decoration; as such, the flavor won't be affected if you can't find it. If you do use it, you must remove the calyx (the green part that holds it together), otherwise it will leave a bitter flavor.

Hierba de conejo can be difficult to source outside of Oaxaca. If you cannot find it, use avocado leaves or sage instead.

————————

To make the frijolón, clean the beans of any debris, rinse, and soak them overnight.

Drain the beans and cook in a large pot along with the onion, garlic, and enough water to cover them by at least 2 inches. Once the water begins to boil, lower the heat, cover the pot, and let the beans cook over medium heat for approximately 3 to 5 hours. Make sure the beans are always covered with water by at least 1 inch, adding more hot water as necessary. The cooked beans will squish easily when pressed between your fingers. Once they are fully cooked, add a teaspoon of salt and boil for another 15 minutes. Drain, reserving the broth, and remove and discard the pieces of cooked onion and garlic.

(recipe continues)

Serves 4

Time: 12 hours to soak the frijolón, 3-5 hours to prep, 45 minutes to cook

For the frijolón

1 cup frijolón, or black beans

⅓ red onion

2 cloves garlic

Water to cover

1 teaspoon salt

For the soup

½ cup red onion, roughly chopped

4 tablespoons vegetable oil or lard (divided)

1 cup fresh hierba de conejo (or substitute avocado leaves or sage)

1½ cups chicken or vegetable stock or water

Salt to taste

To serve

½ cup vegetable oil

4 tortillas, cut into strips

2 tablespoons fresh hierba de conejo (or substitute avocado leaves or sage)

Salt

2 tablespoons cubed queso fresco (or feta cheese)

To make the soup, sauté the red onion in a pan with 2 tablespoons of oil or lard, until it is translucent and begins to burn at the edges. Add the hierba de conejo and cook for another 2 minutes, making sure it does not burn.

Place 2 cups of the cooked beans, the red onion, the hierba de conejo, and 1 cup of the bean broth into a blender. Process until smooth, strain, and set aside.

Place a stock pot over medium-high heat and add the remaining 2 tablespoons of oil or lard. Pour in the bean mixture along with 1½ cups of stock or water, and bring to a boil. Lower the heat to a simmer and cook for 6 to 8 minutes. The consistency is correct when the soup coats the back of a spoon and a line remains visible when a finger is dragged across it. Taste for salt and set aside.

To serve, heat half a cup of vegetable oil in a pan and fry the tortilla strips. Once they are golden and crunchy, remove and set on a paper towel. Use the same oil to fry the hierba de conejo and, once crisp, set next to the tortilla strips. Sprinkle both with salt while they are still hot.

At Casa Oaxaca, this soup is ladled out at the table, so the hot soup is first poured into a terra-cotta pitcher. Arrange a pile of fried tortilla strips in a bowl, sprinkle about 1 tablespoon of queso fresco (or feta cheese) over them, along with a couple of fried hierba de conejo leaves. Scatter the avocado over this and decorate with the blossoms and dried chile, if using. At the table, pour the soup over the garnish.

¼ avocado, shaped into rosettes

½ cup frijolón blossoms for garnish (optional)

Julienned dried chile (optional)

THE JEWEL OF LA CHINANTLA

Caldo de piedra (stone soup) is a pre-Hispanic dish, originally from the municipality of San Felipe Usila (in Nahuatl: huitzila, "where hummingbirds abound") in Tuxtepec, in northern Oaxaca state. The region, with its dazzling foliage, is also known as "La Chinantla" and is mostly inhabited by the Chinantecos, who claim never to have been conquered by the Spanish. It is crossed by the Usila River, which is favorable for fishing.

The traditional preparation of caldo de piedra happens at the river's banks, taking advantage of the natural concavities in the rocks, hollowed by the currents, as cooking vessels. This is a soup offered to the women of the community as a symbol of devotion and thanks, so its preparation is always done by men. Caldo de piedra also represents love for your neighbor, unity, and a form of collective work.

The tasks for its preparation are divided among the participants. One group is dedicated to fishing, scaling, and cleaning, another to the selection and gathering of round stones and oak firewood, while another tends the fire to heat the stones, which become red-hot after a couple of hours and are set down in the riverbank's concavities, now filled with water, fish, freshwater shrimp, tomatoes, onions, and chopped herbs—which could be cilantro, hoja santa, epazote, or a combination of those. The high temperature of the stones from the fire makes the water come to a rolling boil so that the seafood cooks right there, taking on a mineral flavor.

At Casa Oaxaca, we serve a version of a caldo de piedra as a homage to this Chinanteco delicacy.

THE TOOLS OF OUR KITCHEN

Donde hay fogón,
Baila San Pascual Bailón
Otorgando la mejor sazón

Mixe grandmothers say that when the end of the world comes, our pots and comales will attack us in revenge for having burned them while we lived. The only implement that will weep for us is the metate, the stone on which corn and other ingredients are traditionally ground, since we feed that one all our lives.

The tejolote (stone pestle) and the metate (large, flat stone for grinding ingredients) are considered mother and son; in fact, many of the indigenous languages that exist in Mexico designate them as such. The metate is the grindstone, the starring utensil in the meals of our heritage, not only for the unparalleled flavor it lends to foods ground upon it, but because the metate is a symbol in itself.

At the tianguis (open-air street markets) and markets of Oaxaca you'll always find a stand, generally outdoors, that exhibits its metates and molcajetes for sale, in all sizes, with many kinds of decorations carved on them. If you show interest in one, you'll be invited to try it, grinding a handful of corn kernels in the appropriate posture: kneeling on a piece of cardboard.

It's common in many towns for the mother of the bride or the madrina de la boda—the godmother of the marriage—to give the couple their metate. As it is to last a lifetime, it must be chosen with care and then seasoned before it is used. Metates are also passed down, and the inheritance seems to include the seasoning of the woman who left it as her legacy.

Metates, molcajetes, tejolotes, and chilmoleras, descendants of ancestral grindstones, are used to create salsas, masa, and pastes that go into diverse Mexican dishes, but they are also used to blend herbs, seeds, grains, and barks that become the most astonishing dyes for silks, linens, and cottons that are made into thread for the weaving of clothing and textiles.

Kitchen tools are extensions of the body that we have fabricated since ancient times to assist us in preparing our foods. A salsa made in a molcajete will never be the same as a salsa made in a blender. But this more recent invention certainly makes it easier to grind large quantities when necessary.

Tortillas puff better on a clay comal, and there's nothing like the hot chocolate whose foam rises from an expertly applied molinillo (the specialized tool used to mix and foam it) or the dexterity needed to make enormous rolls of masa with beans to later become tamales for the Day of the Dead festivities in Oaxaca's Sierra Norte.

The fogón, the simple construction where a fire is made for cooking, is a primal cooking instrument. In many communities, when a house is built, the first thing planned is the location of the fogón, with its three stones that together form the home's hearth. Over the fogón food will be cooked, curative potions will be brewed, dreams will be shared, and wisdom and culinary customs will be passed down.

In the countryside, the workday begins and ends at the fogón. When putting out the fire, it's said that all the objects in the kitchen should be cleaned, placed upside down, and covered. It is believed that, if they see light, they could come to life during the night and make mischief. This is why metates, comales, pots, and molcajetes are put to bed, just like people: they need to sleep in order to work the following day.

HEIRLOOM TOMATO SALAD

This dish is meant to showcase the many kinds of tomatoes that grow and are used in Oaxacan cooking. The base of the dressing is juice from the tomatoes themselves, to bring out their flavors even further. If you can't find these varieties, you can use others, keeping in mind that the best moment to make this salad is at the height of tomato season.

In Oaxaca, the most commonly available variety is the tomate riñón. This is a traditional variety not associated with large-scale commercial agriculture or what in the United States is called "heirloom." It is meaty, sweet, and extremely delicate, which makes it difficult to export. Similar in flavor to those used in Italy to make a classic Caprese salad, it only takes a little salt and olive oil to make it extraordinary.

The purple miltomate and the cuatomate are small tomatoes that grow among the corn in the milpa.

The pan dulce, or pan mollete, used in this dish is sweetened with piloncillo, an unrefined cane sugar, has anise seeds in the dough, and is occasionally dusted with sesame seeds. If you can't find it, substitute a similar yolk-based bread or baguette.

Take the guaje, guajillo, or Roma tomatoes and cut a large X at the bottom of each one. Place a strainer over a bowl and using your hands squeeze the tomatoes, extracting the seeds and juice. Take care not to break the fruit apart too much. Discard the seeds, save the juices, and set the tomatoes aside.

Add the garlic, lime juice, vinegar, olive oil, basil, and salt to the reserved tomato juices. Stir until the salt is dissolved.

Cut the riñón or heirloom tomatoes and the reserved, squeezed guaje tomatoes into medium-large segments and place them in the bowl with the other tomatoes and tomatillos. Pour the dressing over the tomatoes and toss until they are all covered.

To serve, pile a few tomatoes on each plate, making sure that all the varieties are visible. Pour any leftover dressing over them and arrange the cheese between the chunks. Sprinkle with chia and pumpkin seeds, and garnish with whole fresh basil leaves, tomatillo, and toasted slices of bread.

Serves 4

Time: 30 minutes

4 tomatoes (guaje, guajillo, or Roma)

4 small cloves garlic, finely chopped

2 tablespoons fresh lime juice

1 tablespoon red wine vinegar

¼ cup extra virgin olive oil

10 fresh basil leaves, sliced into strips

1 tablespoon salt

4 riñón tomatoes (or any red heirloom variety)

4 green tomatillos, thinly sliced

4 purple miltomates or heirloom tomatillos, thinly sliced

4 rastrojo, cuatomate, milpa, or cherry tomatoes

To serve

1 pound Oaxacan string cheese, cubed

2 tablespoons chia seeds, toasted

2 tablespoons pumpkin seeds, toasted

20 fresh basil leaves

1 green tomatillo, thinly sliced

1 pan mollete or half a baguette, thinly sliced and toasted

CEVICHE-STUFFED CHILE DE AGUA IN PASSION FRUIT SALSA

To make the chiles, boil 2 cups of water and dissolve the sugar in it. Pour this water into a bowl and add 1 to 2 cups ice. Set aside.

In a small to medium saucepan, heat the vegetable oil. Take the chiles de agua and, using a knife, make a 1-inch incision in the concave side of their curve. This will keep the chiles from bursting open in the hot oil. Submerge the chiles into the oil one by one, leaving them fully covered (add oil if necessary). Cook for 10 to 15 seconds, or until the skin separates and changes from a bright green to a whitish color. Use tongs or a slotted spoon to remove them from the oil and place them in the sweet ice-water bath for about 5 minutes.

Using gloves, peel off the chile skins and cut them lengthwise, starting from the earlier cut. Remove the hearts with all their seeds and veins, taking care not to break them apart too much. Rinse the chiles and place them back in the sweetened water for 10 to 12 minutes. Drain and set aside.

To make the salsa, place the passion fruit pulp in a medium saucepan along with the sugar, cinnamon, and 2 cups of water. Bring to a boil, then lower the heat and simmer until reduced by half, around 35 to 40 minutes. The sauce should become thick, almost like molasses. Remove and discard the cinnamon. Set aside to cool.

To make the ceviche, mix the lime juice, olive oil, oregano, and salt in a glass or nonreactive bowl. Stir until the salt is dissolved. Add the fish and make sure it's completely covered by the lime juice mixture. Refrigerate for about 15 minutes or until the fish looks opaque but not chalky.

Add the mango, tomato, onion, and cilantro to the fish. Toss to mix and taste for salt. Stuff the chiles with the ceviche. To maintain the chiles' shape, cup them in your hand as you fill, and squeeze lightly, compressing the mixture. Once stuffed, return the chiles to the refrigerator for at least 1 hour, or until ready to serve.

To serve, place a couple of spoonfuls of salsa in the center of each plate, then set a chile over the pool of salsa and decorate with pomegranate seeds, cilantro sprouts, and a sweet potato chip. When eating the chile, make sure to cut into it and mix everything together in order to get a balance of the chile's spiciness and the tangy sweetness of the fruit.

Serves 4
Time: 3 hours

For the chiles
2 cups water
1 cup sugar
Ice, as needed
2 cups vegetable oil, plus more as needed
4 chiles de agua (or substitute chiles Anaheim or poblano)

For the salsa
6 passion fruit, pulp scooped out
6 tablespoons sugar
1 cinnamon stick
2 cups water

For the ceviche
1 cup fresh lime juice
¼ cup olive oil
1 teaspoon dried oregano
1 tablespoon salt
1 pound fresh, skinless mahi-mahi, cut into ½-inch dice
¾ cup mango, cut into ½-inch dice
½ cup tomato, seeds removed and cut into ½-inch dice
½ cup finely chopped onion
¼ cup chopped fresh cilantro

To serve
½ cup pomegranate seeds (for garnish)
Cilantro sprouts (for garnish)
4 sweet potato chips (page 118) (for garnish)

A TROVE OF TALENT

Good cooking relies on good vendors, good ingredients, good recipes, etc. But perhaps the most necessary thing is the good attitude of the cooks. My kitchens are happy places where much is learned and where opportunities arise for those who show effort and willingness. The cooks grow, continually facing new challenges and taking responsibility for their work. These are kitchens that teach collaboration, how to lend a hand to someone new and to enjoy the successes of a colleague. My cooks go on to work in other restaurants, inspired and sure of themselves.

For example, the audacious Manuel Baños was the head chef of Casa Oaxaca. Today he is the chef of neighboring restaurant Pitiona, where his talent is on full display. Manolo's cooking is a wild fantasy brought to life on each plate. Another singular example is Luis Arellano, who was in charge of moles in my kitchens and later was the head of the kitchen at Enrique Olvera's Pujol. Today Luis is the chef of Criollo, in the Oaxacan capital.

The same goes for the budding talents. The current heads of the kitchens, at both the restaurant and the hotel, will undoubtedly be among the culinary stars of the future, beginning perhaps with Rafael Villalobos, the chef at Hotel Casa Oaxaca. Rafa is a disciplined and ambitious cook, but above all, he is discerning. His cooking carries his stamp, sometimes delicate and sometimes surprising. He is also my right hand, my second in command.

Odilón García, the current head of the kitchen for the restaurant's evening shift, is also a chef whose career should be followed. Odilón is a soldier of a cook, with an impressive ability to control his stress and work under pressure. This talent is beyond important at Casa Oaxaca—it is necessary, given the quantity of people served during the high season and at private events.

Israel Sosa is another extremely young and talented cook from the Casa Oaxaca camp. Gavilán, as everyone calls him, is the head of the kitchen during the morning shift, always smiling and one of the most trustworthy men to have walked the earth. He is meticulous in his work, a sort of sushi chef. A rare specimen that is very useful in a Oaxacan kitchen.

Finally, I must mention Carlos Galán, the head cook at Guzina Oaxaca, the restaurant I run in Mexico City. Charly is a seasoned cook and very distinguished for someone his age. When I named him head of the kitchen at Guzina, whose diners tend to be knowledgeable and demanding, it was an enormous vote of confidence, one Charly has more than repaid.

My cooks are talented, hardworking people I trust implicitly: people I can rely on so that the restaurants continue to be places of innovation and, at the same time, transmitters of culinary traditions—so that they always feel like casas oaxaqueñas.

SHRIMP, NOPAL, FAVA BEAN, AND PEA SOUP

The dried shrimp give this soup a unique, complex flavor; however, dried shrimp can be quite salty, so be sure to taste for salt and adjust as needed at each step.

_____

Preheat the oven to 250°F.

To make the soup, in a small saucepan boil the dried shrimp with 1½ cups of water for about 20 minutes. Blend in a blender, strain, and set stock aside.

Place the nopal paddles on a baking sheet and bake for 20 minutes, or until their intense green color turns olive. Cut into ½-inch cubes and set aside.

Heat the olive oil in a large, heavy saucepan over medium-high heat. Sauté the onion and garlic until translucent. Add the tomatoes and cook for 2 minutes, then add the fava beans. Stir the mixture together with a wooden spoon, and use the back of the spoon to press the fava beans against the sides of the pan to break them up. You're looking for a chunky purée that will thicken the soup. Add the vegetable or chicken broth, the reserved shrimp stock, and the epazote leaves, and let simmer for 15 minutes. Taste for salt and process in a blender until smooth. Strain and pour into a pitcher to serve at the table.

To serve, place two blanched shrimp into each serving bowl along with some reserved, diced nopales, diced tomatoes, fava beans, and peas.

Garnish with spring onion and chile serrano, the epazote leaves, and the cilantro sprouts and flowers. Pour the soup at the table and serve with lime wedges.

Serves 4

Time: 2 hours

For the soup

¼ cup dried shrimp

1½ cups water

4 nopal (cactus) paddles

3 tablespoons olive oil

1 cup onion, roughly chopped

3 cloves garlic, chopped

3 guajillo or Roma tomatoes, roughly chopped

1 cup cooked fava beans (densely packed)

4 cups vegetable or chicken broth

2 tablespoons epazote leaves, roughly chopped (or 2 teaspoons dried, if fresh is not available)

Salt to taste

To serve

8 large shrimp, blanched

½ guajillo or Roma tomato, seeds removed, diced into ¼-inch cubes

20 fresh green fava beans, blanched and peeled

½ cup peas, blanched

To garnish

1 spring onion head, sliced into thin rounds

½ chile serrano, sliced into thin rounds

Fresh, whole epazote leaves

Fresh cilantro sprouts and flowers

1 lime, quartered

MOLE COLORADITO

Coloradito is a mole from the central valley, similar to mole negro. Its hue comes from the chiles, which retain their color because they are toasted less than in a mole negro, for which you have to char them.

This mole goes well with fatty meats such as pork or duck.

_____

In a small saucepan, place the tomatoes, ¼ cup vegetable oil, and 1 cup of water. Cook for 30 to 35 minutes, or until most of the water has evaporated and the tomatoes begin to come apart. Set tomatoes aside in a large bowl.

Clean the dry chiles with a damp kitchen towel. Preheat a comal or a well-seasoned cast-iron skillet or griddle. Stem and devein all the chiles and discard their seeds.

Toast the chiles over medium heat for about 10 minutes, or until they begin to give off a toasty aroma but retain their color. Set in the bowl with the tomatoes.

Toast the almonds, peanuts, pecans, and sesame seeds until all are lightly browned. Place in the bowl.

In a skillet with a drizzle of oil, sauté the garlic and onion until they turn translucent and are burnt at the edges. Place in the bowl.

In the same skillet, fry the raisins and prunes, bread, plantain, dried thyme, rosemary, oregano, marjoram, cloves, allspice berries, anise seeds, cinnamon stick, and nutmeg. Each ingredient should be fried separately, adding oil as necessary. You are looking to lightly brown the ingredients. Reserve everything in the large bowl as you go.

Working in batches, place a handful of the cooked ingredients and the ginger into a blender or food processor. Set tomatoes at the bottom of each batch, and add water as needed for smoother blending. It is important to ensure that all the ingredients are completely ground.

In a large stock pot or Dutch oven, heat the remaining 1 cup of vegetable oil until it glistens and begins to smoke. Fry the mole sauce over low heat, stirring constantly, for 30 minutes. During this time, incorporate the chocolate, sugar, and salt. Keep stirring to avoid scorching. The water will evaporate and the sauce will turn into a paste. You'll know it's ready when

(recipe continues)

Makes 1 pound mole paste (12 to 15 servings when reconstituted with stock)

Time: 2 hours 30 minutes

3 tomatoes (4 if they are small), preferably guajillo or Roma

¼ cup vegetable oil (plus more for sautéing) and 1 cup for frying the paste

1 cup water, plus more as needed for blending

3 chiles guajillo

3 chiles pasilla

3 chiles anchos

2 chiles meco

2 tablespoons almonds

½ cup peanuts

1 tablespoon pecans

2 tablespoons sesame seeds

3 cloves garlic, sliced

½ medium onion, sliced

1 tablespoon raisins

3 seedless prunes

1 pan amarillito (a dinner-roll-size piece of stale brioche or white bread will do)

1 ripe plantain, peeled and cut into thick slices

1 tablespoon dried thyme

1 tablespoon dried rosemary

a spoon dragged slowly across the bottom of the pan leaves a groove—this may take 45 minutes to 1 hour.

The paste may be stored at this point (mole paste can last for several months in the freezer) or, if it will be eaten immediately, move on to the following steps.

The mole paste can now be turned into a sauce for serving. Chicken, beef, pork, or vegetable stock are all good options for reconstituting it. You will need approximately 3 cups of stock for ½ pound of mole. It is best to use well-seasoned stock and add ¼ cup at a time. The consistency of the finished sauce should be thick, not runny; it should generously coat the back of a spoon.

When the paste is frozen and reconstituted, it's possible to detect very pleasant notes of aging, different from the flavors of recently made paste. Mole paste can be frozen for up to three months.

1 tablespoon dried oregano

1 tablespoon dried marjoram

4 whole cloves

4 allspice berries

1 pinch anise seeds

1 cinnamon stick (about 4 inches long)

¼ teaspoon freshly grated nutmeg

1 slice peeled fresh ginger (about 3 inches long and ¹⁄₁₆ inch thick), roughly chopped

1 cup Oaxacan chocolate, roughly chopped (or substitute semi-sweet chocolate plus ½ teaspoon cinnamon powder and 1 drop of almond extract)

½ cup sugar

½ teaspoon salt

Chicken, beef, pork, or vegetable stock, as needed

DUCK FOR TACOS AND GARNACHAS

Home cooks can feel daunted facing a whole duck for the first time, and yet it's a good exercise in nose-to-tail cooking. When buying a whole duck, be sure to make good use of all of it. Whatever is left from making the garnachas is great for stock that you can use to reconstitute the mole paste you'll be eating with the duck tacos on page 145.

Makes 2 cups duck meat

Time: 3 hours 30 minutes

1 cleaned duck
½ onion
5 cloves garlic
1 small bunch fresh
  thyme
2 tablespoons salt
Water to cover

Cut off the duck's neck and wings; reserve to make stock at a later time. Cut off the duck's legs and place them in a large stockpot along with the torso, onion, garlic, thyme, and 1 tablespoon of salt. Add enough water to cover everything completely.

Bring to a boil, then turn down the heat, cover, and leave to simmer for 3 hours, or until the duck meat falls from the bone. Remove the duck and let cool. Strain the stock and reserve.

Remove all the meat from the bones and then finely chop it along with the skin. It should be chopped to the point of almost becoming a paste. Place the meat in a bowl and add ¼ cup of the stock in which the duck was cooked, and a tablespoon of salt, or more if needed. Mix to combine and reserve to make tacos or garnachas.

The cooked duck meat will keep in the refrigerator for a couple of days and about three months in the freezer. Be sure to wrap it as airtight as possible. To use, thaw completely and reheat in a pan. Cover with a lid and watch carefully to avoid overdrying.

DUCK TACOS WITH MOLE COLORADITO

With your cooked duck (page 143) and the mole coloradito (page 140) on hand, preparing these tacos is quick and easy. We usually serve them as appetizers, but if you want to make a main course out of them, just double the quantities. The mole coloradito is a perfect pairing with the duck's hearty flavor.

_____

Preheat a large skillet and pour in the vegetable oil. Fill the tortillas with the cooked duck and roll them up. Fry the tacos, placing the side where the tortilla closes facedown in the pan. This will ensure that the taco is properly sealed, preventing the filling from spilling out. Cook the tacos for a few minutes, turning them over so that they brown evenly. Once they are golden and crisp, remove and set to drain on a paper towel.

In a small saucepan, dissolve the coloradito paste with the duck stock (or whatever stock you have on hand) and let it simmer over low heat until the sauce is thick, about 12 minutes.

To serve, cut the tacos in half. On each plate serve two tablespoons of beans and place three taco halves on top of them. Bathe with mole and crema, then sprinkle with cheese, and garnish with red onion and cilantro.

Serves 4

Time: 30 minutes

¼ cup vegetable oil

6 corn tortillas (page 11)

1¼ cups duck meat (page 143)

½ cup mole coloradito (page 140)

½ cup stock in which the duck cooked (or other stock)

½ cup hot frijoles de la olla (page 39)

¼ cup crema

¼ cup crumbled queso fresco (or feta cheese)

¼ cup julienned red onion

¼ cup cilantro leaves

CATCH OF THE DAY WITH TOMATO JAM

The pesca del día, the catch of the day, is common throughout the restaurant culture of Mexico, but for me, it has a personal significance. During the time I lived in Puerto Escondido, the catch of the day could mean the only thing I had to eat. My friends and I would go out to sea during the earliest hours of the day. We would take whatever we caught (the catch of the day is nothing more than whatever takes the bait, by chance or destiny) and go back to the beach tired and hungry. There women who ran small restaurants would cook the fish and together we enjoyed the sea's generosity.

The tomato jam is one of my more recent creations, made with the diners at the restaurant and the hotel in mind.

───────────

Preheat the oven to 350°F. To make the jam, bring 2 quarts of water to a boil. Cut an X in the bottom of each tomato, and fill a container with ice-cold water. Once the water reaches a rolling boil, blanch the tomatoes for about 30 seconds, then place them in the ice bath. Peel away the tomato skins. Cut the tomatoes in half, and use your fingers to remove the heart (seeds and ribs). Reserve the flesh and purée the heart and juices. Strain and set aside.

Place the tomatoes in a baking dish or pan, along with the rosemary sprigs and honey, and sprinkle with salt. Bake for 15 minutes. Remove from the oven and place everything in the baking dish (including any juices) into a saucepan. Add the puréed tomato to the saucepan and cook over low heat for about 1 hour, or until most of the liquid evaporates and the mixture takes on the thick consistency of jam. Remove and discard the rosemary sprigs and set aside.

To make the garlic oil, in a blender place the olive oil and garlic cloves (it is not necessary to peel them). Process, strain, and set it aside. If making in advance, store the garlic oil in the fridge.

To make the fish: Once the oven is at 350°F, use a paper towel to dry the fish fillets. Season them with salt and pepper. In an ovenproof pan, heat the olive oil over medium heat until it becomes shiny and just begins to smoke. Fry the fish, placing it skin-side down first, and leave it there

(recipe continues)

Serves 4

Time: 2 hours 45 minutes

For the jam

2 quarts water (for blanching)

10 guajillo or Roma tomatoes

3 fresh rosemary sprigs

¼ cup honey

1 teaspoon salt

For the garlic oil

½ cup olive oil

½ whole head of garlic

For the fish

4 6-ounce fresh sea bass or red snapper fillets, skin on

Salt and pepper to taste

¼ cup olive oil

¼ cup garlic oil (recipe above)

½ cup capers

½ cup fresh lime juice

To serve

12 leaves ruby red lettuce (or any other red-colored lettuce)

4 tablespoons cold unsalted butter

2 tablespoons capers (to garnish)

4 squash blossoms, petals only (to garnish)

without moving it for 4 to 5 minutes. The pan should be large enough to leave space between each fillet; crowding the pan will prevent the skin from crisping.

Once the skin is golden brown and it's easy to move the fillets, turn them over and add the garlic oil, capers, and lime juice. Place the pan in the oven to finish cooking, about 5 to 8 minutes, depending on the thickness of the fillets.

To serve, lay three lettuce leaves on each plate, spoon some jam over them, and set the fillets on top. Once you remove the fillets from the pan, add the butter to the remaining juices and stir until it emulsifies. Bathe each fish with this sauce. Garnish with capers and squash blossom petals. Serve immediately.

GRILLED OCTOPUS WITH HOJA SANTA PESTO

The hoja santa pesto in this recipe is my Mexican version of the classic Italian sauce; here, the hoja santa and parsley replace the basil, and the pumpkin seeds stand in for pine nuts. Like all good pestos, this one is very versatile. If you have any left over, serve it with pasta, seafood, or as a dressing for vegetables.

The rice with huitlacoche is also reminiscent of another Italian classic: risotto. The huitlacoche brings balance to this dish.

———————————

To make the octopus, set it in a large pot with enough water to cover. Add the garlic, onion, bay leaves, allspice, and salt. Bring water to a boil, then lower the heat to a simmer. Cook for 1 to 2 hours. You'll know the octopus is ready when a knife inserted into the thickest part of a tentacle slides in easily. Place the octopus in an ice-water bath for 5 minutes to stop it cooking. Drain and set aside in the refrigerator.

To make the pesto, place the onion, garlic, pumpkin seeds, allspice, and olive oil into a blender. Process for 3 to 4 minutes, scraping down the sides as needed, until everything is completely ground. Add the parsley, hoja santa, and salt and blend until a smooth paste is formed. Set pesto aside.

To make the rice, place a saucepan over medium heat. Add 3 tablespoons of oil and brown the rice, stirring continuously for 5 to 8 minutes, or until golden. In a blender, along with ½ cup of stock or water, place the whole clove of garlic, the ⅓ onion, and 1 teaspoon of salt. Process and add to the saucepan. Cook until the liquid evaporates. Pour in the remaining ½ cup of stock or water and bring to a boil. Once it boils, turn down the heat, add the parsley, cover with a lid, and leave to simmer for about 30 minutes.

To make the huitlacoche, preheat a large cast-iron skillet. Add 1 tablespoon of vegetable oil and sauté the garlic and the 1 tablespoon of minced onion until translucent. Add the huitlacoche, turn the heat to low, cover, and cook for 5 minutes. Add the epazote and the teaspoon of salt, mix, and set aside. Just before serving, over medium heat, fold in the rice, crema, and cheese.

(recipe continues)

Serves 4

Time: 2 hours
30 minutes

For the octopus
1 2-pound octopus, head removed
Water to cover
4 cloves garlic
½ white onion
6 bay leaves
5 allspice berries
1 teaspoon salt

For the pesto
⅓ cup white onion, roughly chopped
2 cloves garlic
½ cup unsalted pumpkin seeds, toasted
2 allspice berries
1 cup olive oil
½ cup parsley, roughly chopped
½ cup hoja santa, roughly chopped
1 tablespoon salt

For the rice
3 tablespoons vegetable oil
½ cup white rice, rinsed and drained
1 clove garlic
⅓ onion
1 teaspoon salt
1 cup stock or water
1 stalk parsley

To make the grilled vegetables, steam them until a knife slides in easily. Cook the beet separately so that it won't stain the other vegetables. Place the zucchini, carrot, and chayote in a bowl and add olive oil and salt, turning to coat completely. Remove them from the bowl, set aside, add the beet, and coat with the remaining oil.

Remove the octopus from the fridge 30 minutes before serving. Preheat a well-oiled grill or cast-iron skillet on the highest setting. Place the octopus in a bowl, pour the pesto over it, and stir to make sure it's completely covered. Grill for 5 minutes on each side, until it forms a browned crust. The octopus can be grilled whole or divided into servings; what's important is that the grill or skillet be very hot so that a crunchy crust forms quickly without overcooking the meat.

Grill the vegetables on a very hot grill or grill pan until they have grill marks on each side. It's wise to roast the beet last and keep it separate until the moment the dish is served.

Place some huitlacoche rice at the center of each plate, then set the octopus and the vegetables around it. Garnish with fresh purslane leaves and red onion.

For the huitlacoche

1 tablespoon vegetable oil

1 clove garlic, chopped

1 tablespoon minced white onion

¾ cup (packed) huitlacoche

1 tablespoon finely chopped epazote (or 1 teaspoon dried)

1 teaspoon salt

½ cup crema

¼ cup crumbled queso istmeño or aged cotija

For the grilled vegetables

1 zucchini, cut diagonally into 4 pieces

1 carrot, peeled, cut diagonally into 4 pieces

1 chayote (mirliton), peeled, cut in half lengthwise, then diagonally into 4 pieces

¼ cup olive oil

1 tablespoon salt

1 beet, peeled, cut in half crosswise, then diagonally into 4 pieces

To serve

¼ cup verdolagas (purslane) (to garnish)

Thinly sliced red onion (to garnish)

GUAJILLO SHRIMP WITH CHAYOTE AND PLANTAIN PURÉE

The sauce and the saltiness in this recipe come mostly from the brine of the capers, so it's important to add it little by little and to taste for salt at each step. You must also take into account that different kinds of capers will vary in their saltiness, so try them before you begin cooking.

To make the purée, melt the butter in a large sauté pan or cast-iron skillet, add the plantain, and mash it. Stir in the chayote and continue mashing to arrive at a chunky purée. Add salt and set aside.

To make the shrimp, in another large pan or cast-iron skillet heat the olive oil. Once hot, add the red onion and garlic, sautéing until they turn translucent. Add the shrimp, capers, mushrooms, chile guajillo, lime juice, and stock. Cook for 2 minutes. Add a splash of the brine from the capers and the butter, then taste for salt. The shrimp are cooked when they turn from translucent to opaque white.

Place a spoonful of purée in the middle of each plate and set the shrimp over it, along with some of the sauce left in the pan. Garnish with parsley and onion.

Serves 4

Time: 30 minutes

For the purée

2 tablespoons unsalted butter

1 cup plantain (very ripe, almost black), cut into small dice (1 large plantain)

1 cup chayote (mirliton), boiled and cut into small dice (about 2 chayotes)

1 teaspoon salt

For the shrimp

¼ cup olive oil

½ cup red onion, sliced

4 cloves garlic, thinly sliced

20 large shrimp, peeled and deveined

¼ cup capers, brine reserved

½ cup mushrooms (oyster or cremini are ideal), chopped

1 chile guajillo, sliced, seeds removed

1 tablespoon fresh lime juice

½ cup fish, chicken, or vegetable stock

4 tablespoons unsalted butter

To garnish

1 tablespoon parsley, chopped

1 tablespoon onion, thinly sliced

GRILLED STEAKS WITH CHAPULÍN SALSA

At Casa Oaxaca, we think of this sauce as the ideal way to introduce the particular flavor of chapulines—grasshoppers—to diners without confronting them with the challenge of eating insects. The sauce balances the nutty flavor of the chapulines with the smokiness of the chile morita and the acidity of the miltomates.

———————

To make the salsa, heat the vegetable oil in a medium skillet over medium-high heat. Sauté the onion and garlic. Once the onion turns translucent and begins to brown at the edges, add the chapulines and the chile morita, along with the liquid in which the chiles were hydrated. Cook for 2 minutes. Add the miltomates, cilantro, and beef stock and bring to a boil. Turn the heat down to medium-low and simmer for 5 minutes. Add the vinegar, incorporating it a tablespoon at a time and tasting after each addition until you reach the desired acidity, considering the chapulines and the miltomates will also add to the tartness. Cook for 2 more minutes, then add salt to taste. Pour into a blender, process, strain, and reserve. When reheating sauce to serve, reduce once more over low heat until it thickens slightly.

To make the sweet potato purée, preheat the oven to 400°F. Prick the sweet potatoes all over with a fork. Place them on a baking sheet and bake for 45 minutes to 1 hour, turning over once, until the potatoes are soft and cooked through. Remove from oven and set aside until cool enough to handle. Cut each potato in half and scoop out the flesh with a spoon. Discard the skins. Place the sweet potato pulp into a food processor along with the butter, sour cream, and salt. Blend until smooth and set aside. To reheat for serving, place purée in a pan over medium heat and add milk by the tablespoon.

To make the scallions, coat them with olive oil and salt. Roast over a hot grill or grill pan until softened and charred in parts.

To make the steaks, if they were refrigerated, take them out and let them come to room temperature. Heat a large cast-iron skillet. Rub the steaks all over with olive oil and season generously with salt and pepper. Add steaks to skillet and cook over medium-high heat for about 4 min-

Serves 4
Time: 1 hour 45 minutes

For the salsa

2 tablespoons vegetable oil

⅓ cup onion, cut into thick wedges

2 cloves garlic

½ cup chapulines

1 chile morita soaked in ½ cup hot water (soaking water reserved)

10 miltomates or tomatillos, roasted

3 fresh cilantro sprigs

½ cup beef stock

¼ cup apple cider vinegar

Salt, to taste

For the sweet potato purée

1½ pounds whole sweet potatoes (approximately 4 potatoes), washed, unpeeled

2 tablespoons butter

3 tablespoons sour cream

1 teaspoon salt

¼ cup milk (for reheating)

For the roasted scallions

8 whole scallions

¼ cup olive oil

1 teaspoon salt

utes, until a brown crust has formed. Turn steaks and cook on the other side for another 4 minutes. Transfer the steaks to a cutting board and let rest for 5 minutes before cutting against the grain into ½-inch slices.

Place a couple of roasted scallions on each plate, and next to them some sweet potato purée, setting the sliced steak on top. Spoon salsa over the steak and serve immediately.

For the steaks
4 7-ounce rib-eye steaks
2 tablespoons olive oil
Salt
Pepper

LAMB CHOPS IN PITIONA SAUCE

Although this dish incorporates traditional Oaxacan ingredients, the techniques are very much influenced by Middle Eastern cooking.

Pitiona has an herbal flavor that is somewhere between oregano and mint, and it gives a spectacular dimension to the lamb. The eggplant purée recalls the taste of baba ganoush, with a silky texture that also complements the lamb. Another way to cook the eggplant and ramp up its smoky notes is to char it directly over a burner. When the skin is blackened and brittle and the eggplant is soft to the touch, cut it in half and scoop out the flesh.

Preheat the oven to 400°F. To begin, place the apples in a baking dish with the cut sides facing up. Coat the eggplants and garlic in olive oil, sprinkle with salt, and place them next to the apples, also cut sides up. Cover the dish with aluminum foil and bake for 20 to 40 minutes, or until the apple, eggplant, and garlic are browned and soft and their skins wrinkled.

To make the apple purée, when the apples are just cool enough to handle, remove and discard the skins. Place the apple pulp in a food processor or blender along with the quince paste, butter, and salt. The apples should still feel hot to the touch as their warmth is vital to help emulsify the mixture. Process until smooth, scraping down the sides as necessary. Reserve and set aside.

To make the eggplant purée, scoop out the eggplants' flesh with a spoon and place it in a food processor or blender. Squeeze the garlic halves into the processor or blender along with the butter, heavy cream, oregano, and lime juice. Process until smooth, adding water by the spoonful if necessary. Be careful not to add too much, as you are looking for a thick purée.

To make the pitiona sauce, heat 1 tablespoon olive oil in a large sauté pan over medium-high heat. Add garlic, onion, and salt and cook, stirring frequently until they soften and start to char at the edges, about 8 to 10 minutes. Add the dried pitiona and cook for 2 more minutes or until the herb has released its aroma. Deglaze the pan with 1 cup of beef stock, scraping up the browned bits at the bottom of the pan. Transfer to a blender along with the remaining 1 cup beef stock, process, and strain

(recipe continues)

Serves 4
Time: 2 hours

To begin
2 Granny Smith apples, halved, not peeled
2 large eggplants, halved lengthwise
1 small head garlic, cut in half crosswise
⅓ cup olive oil
Sprinkle of salt

For the apple purée
12 ounces ate de membrillo (quince paste)
3 tablespoons butter
¼ teaspoon salt

For the eggplant purée
1 tablespoon butter
¼ cup heavy cream
¼ teaspoon ground oregano
½ teaspoon fresh lime juice

For the pitiona sauce
1 tablespoon olive oil
2 cloves garlic, roughly chopped
½ onion, cut into wedges
½ tablespoon salt
2 tablespoons dried pitiona powder
2 cups beef stock, divided

into a small saucepan. Reduce by half over medium heat, about 35 to 40 minutes. In a heavy Dutch oven or cast-iron skillet, melt the butter over medium heat. Add the flour and whisk into the fat, until you reach an amber brown color, about 5 minutes. Add a couple of tablespoons of the pitiona reduction and keep whisking until it is smooth and without lumps. Pour the rest of the pitiona reduction into the skillet and incorporate with the flour mixture. When ready to serve, bring the sauce to a boil, then lower the heat and simmer for about 5 minutes.

To make the lamb, mix 2 tablespoons of the olive oil, the salt, and the pepper in a large bowl. Add lamb and coat completely. Let marinate at room temperature for 30 minutes.

Heat remaining olive oil in a large ovenproof skillet over high heat. When it just begins to smoke, cook the lamb until browned, about 3 minutes per side, working in batches to avoid overcrowding the pan.

When you've browned all the lamb, place it back into the skillet and transfer to the oven. Roast to the desired doneness, about 10 minutes for medium-rare (130°F on an instant-read thermometer). Remove from oven, tent with aluminum foil, and let rest for 5 minutes while you plate.

To make the salad, mix all the ingredients in a bowl. Do this at the last minute to prevent the purslane from wilting.

Place 2 tablespoons of eggplant purée on each plate, along with a few large dots of apple purée, and some salad to the side. Set the lamb over the purées and spoon hot pitiona sauce over it.

1 teaspoon butter

¼ teaspoon flour

For the lamb

¼ cup olive oil, divided

1 tablespoon salt

¼ teaspoon fresh pepper

4 small 4-bone racks of lamb (about ½ pound each)

For the salad

2 cups washed verdolagas (purslane)

2 radishes, thinly sliced

½ tablespoon fresh lime juice

2 tablespoons olive oil

½ teaspoon salt

CHRONICLE OF THE DINERS

To get to my restaurant, Casa Oaxaca, you have to pass in front of the Church of Santo Domingo de Guzmán, with its yellow cantera stone that glows every afternoon in the sunset, sitting peacefully at the highest part of the "Verde Antequera." Santo Domingo is an impressive temple, and a museum with an interior patio whose splendor competes only with that of the neighboring ethnobotanical garden. The streets surrounding the restaurant are the most beautiful in the magnificent colonial city of Oaxaca.

On Calle de la Constitución, a few meters from the stairs of the church's atrium, you will see the facade Casa Oaxaca shares with the Quetzalli gallery next door. For years the wall was a burnt red, but more recently it has been painted sky blue. Both colors work well; the first made you think of the earth, while the current one recalls the heavens. When you enter the restaurant, you first find yourself on a patio with a sculpture and comfortable chairs for drinking mezcal and having a snack. At the back left of the patio is the entrance to the restaurant, which is divided into an interior salon with the main kitchen and an upstairs terrace where most of the tables are, not to mention one of the best views of the city. The Oaxacan sky frames the scene, clean, warm, and dry almost all year long.

Juanita, dressed in a spectacular red huipil (a type of tunic), welcomes you and takes you to the terrace. Florencio greets you affectionately; he already knows you like mezcal and offers you a glass.

On the table are duck garnachas, a salad with tomates riñón and Oaxacan string cheese, stuffed flores de calabaza and xoconostle mezcalinis (page 171), plus a few more mezcals, all accompanied by the sunset, birdsong in the background, and what López Velarde calls Mexico's "countryside with its sleepless clock."

In this way, an afternoon snack becomes a dinner, then a party.

CORN PANQUÉ

To make the panqué, preheat the oven to 400°F. Place the corn, eggs, and evaporated, condensed, and fresh milks into a blender and process until smooth. Pour the mixture into a greased 9×9-inch pan, and cover with greased aluminum foil. Bake in the oven in a water bath for 1½ to 2 hours. Remove from oven and allow to cool. Cut into rectangles and set aside.

To make the lemon verbena cream, bring heavy cream to a simmer in a small saucepan. Remove from heat and add the lemon verbena leaves. Let sit for 15 minutes. Strain into a bowl and let cool for at least 1 hour. Before serving, beat infused cream with 2 tablespoons powdered sugar, until soft peaks form. Set aside.

To make the corn topping, melt the butter in a small skillet and add the blanched corn, sugar, and cinnamon. Cook, stirring occasionally, for 3 to 5 minutes, or until the corn turns golden brown. Set aside.

To make the chile crumble, in a medium bowl combine the flour, brown and granulated sugars, chile powder, and salt. Add the cubed butter and mix it by hand until it forms clumps and crumbs. Cover and refrigerate for 45 minutes. Bake on a sheet pan at 400°F for 10 to 12 minutes, or until it begins to brown. Once cool, break it with your hands into small- to medium-sized crumbs. Set aside.

To make the candied cacao nibs, heat sugar in a small skillet over medium heat, but don't stir it. When it begins to caramelize add the cacao nibs. Stir to combine. All the nibs should be well coated and no sugar grains should remain visible. Make sure not to burn the caramel as it will become bitter. Remove from the heat and spread the cacao over a sheet of parchment paper or aluminum foil. Once it cools, break it up into clusters and set aside.

To serve, place a piece of corn panqué on each plate, then spoon the corn topping over it, as well as some crumble and cacao nibs. Finish off with dots of lemon verbena cream.

Serves 6
Time: 2 hours

For the corn panqué
4 cups fresh corn kernels
6 eggs
1 can evaporated milk
1 can condensed milk
1½ cups milk

For the lemon verbena cream
1 cup heavy cream
¼ cup (packed) lemon verbena leaves
2 tablespoons powdered sugar

For the corn topping
1 tablespoon butter
½ cup fresh corn kernels, rinsed and blanched
1 tablespoon brown sugar
½ teaspoon cinnamon powder

For the chile crumble
¼ cup plus 2 tablespoons wheat flour
2½ tablespoons brown sugar
1 tablespoon granulated sugar
⅛ tablespoon chile powder (or a chile pasilla, deveined, toasted, and ground)
¼ teaspoon salt
3 tablespoons cold butter, cut into cubes

For the candied cacao nibs
1½ tablespoons granulated sugar
¼ cup cacao nibs, toasted

OAXACAN CHOCOLATE MOUSSE

This recipe integrates Mexican ingredients into a very classic dessert. The velvety chocolate mousse is balanced by the acidity of the hibiscus, which in turn is complemented by the fruity caramel tones of the piloncillo. The chile is a smoky, lightly spicy surprise ending, while the sesame seeds, though seemingly just a garnish, contribute another layer of flavor and texture.

Oaxacan chocolate is a mix of toasted cacao, almonds, cinnamon, and sugar. The proportions of these vary greatly, with each brand having its own mix ground at the mill. Because some brands use more sugar than others, taste the Oaxacan chocolate first. If it's too sweet, reduce the amount of sugar in the recipe by up to half. If you can't find Oaxacan chocolate, try substituting with an equal amount of semi-sweet chocolate, and add 1 teaspoon cinnamon powder and 1 drop of almond extract.

To make the mousse, melt the chocolate in a double boiler or a metal bowl set over a pan of simmering water. Stir frequently. Set aside to cool.

In another bowl, beat cream until stiff peaks form. Cover and chill.

In another bowl, beat the egg whites until foamy. Add sugar and keep beating until stiff peaks form.

Fold whipped cream into the chocolate in two parts. Fold egg whites into the chocolate cream mixture, incorporating ¼ of the beaten egg whites first, and continuing with the rest. This will ensure an airy mousse. Refrigerate until firm, at least 2 hours.

Meanwhile, to make the hibiscus reduction, boil the hibiscus flowers, cinnamon, and piloncillo in a small saucepan, along with 1 cup of water. Reduce heat to a simmer and cook for 30 minutes. Strain and boil once again for 15 to 20 minutes or until you obtain syrup with a molasses-like consistency.

To serve, pour some hibiscus syrup onto each plate, scoop some mousse on top, and sprinkle with sesame seeds and chile powder.

Serves 4

Time: 1 hour 30 minutes

For the mousse

7 ounces Oaxacan chocolate

1 cup heavy cream

2 egg whites

2 tablespoons granulated sugar

For the hibiscus reduction

2½ ounces dry hibiscus flowers

1 cinnamon stick

4 ounces by weight piloncillo (or jaggery, muscovado, or turbinado sugar)

1 cup water

To serve

2 tablespoons sesame seeds, toasted

1 chile pasilla, deveined, toasted, and ground into a powder (or substitute store-bought chile powder)

MEZCAL IS THE WAY

The maguey is the tree of wonders . . .
—JOSÉ DE ACOSTA

Mezcal, obtained from assorted different species of maguey, is more than an intoxicating beverage. It is also a symbol of community and work, of power and respect, of enjoyment and celebration. Mezcal links us to the Mexican fields. It is sun, it is time, it is water, resistances, and bonanzas interwoven into a spirit.

Maguey (also known as agave), a plant of wonders, has been a gift from the earth throughout the years. As a botanical species, the maguey presents its greatest biological diversity in the territories of Oaxaca: around thirty varieties, some wild, some domesticated thousands of years ago, are used to make mezcal. Each variety of the plant takes a different amount of time to grow, ranging from seven to twenty-five years, time during which the maguey's sugars and herbaceous flavors accumulate, distinguishing mezcal from any other beverage in the world.

The sensory legacy of mezcal contains a combination of these different agaves with distinct traditions of production. In Oaxaca—the top mezcal-making region in Mexico, bar none—maguey is cooked in an underground stone oven, but each town's mezcal finds its own unique expression; to cook the maguey's heart or piñas—so called because it looks like a piña (pineapple) or pinecone once the pencas (leaves) are cut—to make mezcal, some use acacia wood, mesquite, oak, or pine, while the fermentation tanks may be made of stone, clay, concrete, wood, or animal hides; final distillation is done in copper or clay. If the traditions of each mezcal-making town define a style, the heart of mezcal is its human component: all master mezcal makers bring their own personal heritage to life through their craft. The variables in production are so numerous that you can't say there is one definitive mezcal, but a good mezcal should respect the taste of the maguey of its origin and the hands that made it.

In the mezcal-making towns, before drinking mezcal you must give a few drops to the earth, give it thanks, talk to it, and, of course, give it more if it asks for it. Mezcal is the vehicle of dialogue with supernatural entities.

Mezcal plays various roles in Oaxacan communities; it is therapeutically rubbed on troubled parts of the body and used to cure frights, and in fortune-telling and different ritual practices it serves as a main offering. It is also a gift for shamans, for those who assume a political post or community duty, or to seal alliances such as marriages and the naming of godparents.

As a festive element it's never missing at celebrations. It's the water that makes one joyful, the serum of happiness, magic that sends you on your way.

For hundreds of years this beverage was produced solely for local consumption, but today mezcal has such an aura that I am not surprised it has conquered the palates of chefs, travelers, bartenders, pleasure-seekers, and connoisseurs the world over, nor that today it's a drink appreciated and consumed in every corner of the planet.

We at Casa Oaxaca have been celebrating mezcal culture from the very beginning. From the moment we opened our bar, we have always had four or five artisanal brands of mezcal on hand.

XOCONOSTLE MEZCALINI

Salt the rim of a cold martini glass with sal de gusano. In a cocktail glass or shaker macerate the prickly pear fruit with 4 epazote leaves, crushing them slightly so that they release their juices and aromatic oils. Add the lime and pineapple juices, as well as the simple syrup or sugar and enough ice to fill the glass. Mix well. Add the mezcal. Shake hard and strain into a martini glass. Garnish with a slice of prickly pear and the remaining epazote leaf.

Serves 1

Sal de gusano (worm salt)

1 small xoconostle or prickly pear fruit, peeled and diced into small pieces, plus slice for garnish

4 epazote leaves plus 1 for garnish

½ ounce fresh lime juice

2 ounces fresh pineapple juice

1 ounce simple syrup or 2 teaspoons sugar

2 ounces young mezcal (espadín variety)

TWO PASSIONS MEZCALINI

Salt the rim of a cold martini glass with sal de gusano. Place the apple and lime juice in a cocktail glass or shaker. Crush them or let them macerate, then add the simple syrup or sugar, passion fruit pulp, and enough ice to fill the glass. Add the mezcal. Shake hard and strain into a martini glass. Garnish with an apple slice.

Serves 1

Sal de gusano (worm salt)

⅓ Gala apple, minced, plus slice for garnish

1 ounce fresh lime juice

1½ ounces simple syrup or 3 teaspoons sugar

2½ ounces fresh passion fruit pulp (from puréeing and straining 1 passion fruit)

2 ounces young mezcal (espadín variety)

LIME AGUA FRESCA

In Oaxaca, lime agua fresca is an unusual green color, almost fluorescent, which might seem unnatural. Yet quite the opposite is true: it's made with lime zest as well as the leaves of the lime tree, which give the drink its bright green tone and a deeper, more herbaceous flavor than the best lime agua fresca in the rest of Mexico.

Serves 4 (makes approximately 3 cups)

4 ounces fresh lime juice

2 ounces fresh lime sorbet

6 ounces lime zest

3 lime tree leaves

3 cups water

3 ounces simple syrup or 6 teaspoons white sugar

1 tablespoon chia seeds, lightly toasted

Blend the lime juice, the lime sorbet, the lime zest, and the lime leaves together in a blender until the leaves are disintegrated. Strain and discard the solids. Add 3 cups of water and the simple syrup (or sugar) and mix well. Add the chia seeds and refrigerate until very cold.

PINOLE

In Huautla de Jiménez, Oaxaca, Mazatec cooks prepare this drink with toasted corn, sugar, and cinnamon.

Serves 4 (makes approximately 3 cups)

3 tablespoons toasted corn powder (you can toast and pulverize a couple of corn tortillas)

½ teaspoon cinnamon

2 ounces simple syrup or 4 teaspoons white sugar

3 cups water

Place all the ingredients into a large pitcher and stir until the sugar dissolves. Refrigerate until very cold.

THE PRIVILEGE OF BEING OAXACAN

Cooking is the ultimate expression of a culture. Culinary practices take longer to disappear than clothing or even language. The food traditions one is born into and grows up with remain written on the most elemental parts of memory. Food and cooking unite us, and they are so constant an affirmation that they form a kind of automatic expression of culture and the customs that we share with our families, our regions, and our country.

In a world of contrasts such as ours, cooking is perhaps what most unites us as a people. As nutritional standardization has come to both small towns and cities, and globalization is what's on the tables of both rich and poor, in Oaxaca one eats like a Oaxacan, what is Oaxacan is preserved. The original, natural food and ingredients of this region appeal to all, without distinction.

I am, in the context of global gastronomy, privileged. In an age during which informed consumers try assiduously to avoid fast food and revalue consumption of what's local, native, organic—and what's grown within a few miles from where we will eat it—I did not have to "go back" to my roots, because I never left them. I belong to a society that has safeguarded its flavors and customs, and I have had the opportunity to spearhead a movement that has worked for their promotion, the widening of their expression, to take them to those from afar. I have been able to introduce Oaxacan cooking to a larger audience, to ensure its popularity beyond the borders of Oaxaca, with diners from other latitudes.

Casa Oaxaca opened at the very beginning of what we might call Mexico's emergence on the international culinary stage. What a privilege, then, to be Oaxacan, to grow up where what is authentic, what is one's own, is cultivated and shared.

PART FOUR WHERE I EAT

TULE

MONTE ALBÁN

AEROPUERTO

ZAACHILA

ALLENDE

BRAVO

A

B · ABASOLO

INDEPENDENCIA

2o DE NOV

REFORMA

TEOTITLÁN
DEL VALLE

TLACOLULA

EATING FOR INSPIRATION

A regular day for me involves tending to the stoves in my kitchen and to my customers and talking with my purveyors. I pop in and out among the hotel, the restaurant, the garden at La Raya, and the Mercado de Abastos, the market where I go to buy much of the produce I cook with. In the midst of these comings and goings at the kitchens, the dining rooms, and the markets, comes one of the most important parts of my day: meal time. These are not only moments to rest, but to be inspired by, and to remain connected to, what's most important: food.

I like simple foods best, because they remind me of my childhood and because they contain the touchstones of the Oaxacan palate: memelas, tacos, molotes, barbacoa, and biuses (pork offal), all accompanied with their special salsas. These dishes are prepared throughout Oaxaca by people who, with great care and dedication, labor to preserve the popular and traditional flavors of the regions or towns from which they come. I draw enormous inspiration from these artisans, and here I share just a few of my favorites.

1. TLAMANALLI
Av. Juárez 39, Centro, Teotitlán del Valle, Oaxaca

2. TACOS DEL CARMEN ALTO
Manuel García Vigil on the corner of Quetzalcóatl, Centro, Oaxaca, Oaxaca

3. LA GÜERA DE ABASTOS
Juárez Maza s/n, Mercado de Abastos, Oaxaca, Oaxaca

4. MOLOTES DEL MERCADO REFORMA
Mercado Hidalgo (known as Mercado de la Colonia Reforma),
Palmeras s/n, Reforma, Oaxaca, Oaxaca

5. LA TECA
Violetas 200 A, Reforma, Oaxaca, Oaxaca

6. EL MANGALITO
Cosijoeza 200, La Soledad, Villa de Zaachila, Oaxaca

7. MERCADO DE TLACOLULA
Weekly market, Tercera Sección, Tlacolula de Matamoros, Oaxaca

MY RESTAURANTS

A. CASA OAXACA – THE HOTEL
Manuel García Vigil 407, Centro, Oaxaca, Oaxaca

B. CASA OAXACA – THE RESTAURANT
Av. Gurrión 104 A, Ruta Independencia, Centro, Oaxaca, Oaxaca

C. CASA OAXACA – CAFÉ
Calle Jazmines 518, Reforma, Oaxaca, Oaxaca

I. TLAMANALLI

Av. Juárez 39, Centro, Teotitlán del Valle, Oaxaca

Abigail Mendoza is one of the most well-known and respected traditional cooks in the state of Oaxaca and, indeed, in all of Mexico.

Her family is from Teotitlán del Valle, a region of the central valley known for making artisanal wool rugs and weavings, and now, additionally, as the location of the restaurant where Abigail is the chef: Tlamanalli.

According to Fray Alonso de Molina, author of the sixteenth-century text *Vocabulario en Lengua Castellana y Mexicana,* the word tlamanaliztli means "offering." It makes sense that the name of Abigail's restaurant alludes to an offering. The food she and her sisters prepare is of the rigorous Zapotec tradition, a deeply religious and mystical culture in which offerings are an intrinsic part. Food itself is an offering, an invitation to share the Zapotec culinary tradition that has been transmitted orally, if the story is accurate, for the last 2,500 years. An offering to the living, those who come from afar, those who come hungry.

The restaurant's dining room is a wide-open space decorated with crafts from the region. The kitchen reigns in the middle. There steam emanates from clay pots and comales treated with lime. The women work, dressed in regional clothes, smiling and silent. It is a privilege to sit among them. The daily list of food offered is short, unknown to your average diner. Sopa de chipiles, chicken segueza (stew), mole negro. Everything ground by someone kneeling before a metate.

The level of refinement and sophistication of the food served at Tlamanalli is highly uncommon. In its aromas, there is a distant hum, a glimpse of the ancient, an almost religious dedication. I consider Abigail to be the true ambassador of Oaxaca to the rest of the world. Her legacy is infinite.

2. TACOS DEL CARMEN ALTO

Manuel García Vigil on the corner of Quetzalcóatl, Centro, Oaxaca, Oaxaca

Just two short blocks from Hotel Casa Oaxaca—and also from the Church of Santo Domingo—on the corner of García Vigil and Quetzalcóatl, and a few steps from the temple whose name it borrows, are some of the best street tacos in Oaxaca. It's a very popular stand, success that is well deserved for the quality it has offered for more than forty years, satisfying the cravings of locals and foreigners alike.

When I need a break after a tiring shift, or when I need to lift the energies of my kitchen staff, I usually make a run for these tacos, made with freshly prepared blue corn tortillas and abundant fillings. There are also quesadillas and memelas, but it's best to try the tacos, which are truly special and accompanied by great salsas. There are classic fillings and lesser-known ones: mushrooms, tinga, flor de calabaza (squash blossoms), requesón (ricotta), tasajo encebollado (beef with caramelized onions), chile relleno (stuffed chile poblano), nopales con papa (nopales with potato), salsa de chicharrón (wash pot pork rinds in salsa) . . . It's always tough to choose from their fifteen-plus guisados (stews). If I can only have one taco, though, it would have to be chorizo con quesillo, or spicy pork sausage with Oaxacan string cheese. But the good thing is there's no reason to limit yourself. When you order a taco, the cook pinches off a bit of masa, forms a large tortilla and, once it's cooked, puts the taco together with the chosen guiso (stew), Oaxacan string cheese, if needed, and a special salsa over everything. The seasoning and the price are just right, and when you take into account the generous servings and the stupendous location, Tacos del Carmen Alto is an obligatory stop in the Oaxacan capital.

This is practical food, but not fast food, because even though the guisados are prepared the night before, the tortillas are made to order, and customers always have to stand in line and wait. There are a few benches that would never be enough to accommodate all the diners, but where to sit hardly matters when you finally get your taco. Etiquette calls for dressing it with extra salsa and eating it right away, sitting or standing—who cares when you're eating on one of the prettiest streets in the city?

3. LA GÜERA DE ABASTOS

Juárez Maza s/n, Mercado de Abastos, Oaxaca, Oaxaca

When you shop for groceries at the Mercado de Abastos, the largest market in Oaxaca, recognized as the commercial zone of greatest importance in the city, you can't miss having memelas (masa cakes) and tasajo (thinly sliced grilled flank steak that's been previously cured in salt) for breakfast at La Güera's stand. There's always a risk that she will run out of meat, which is why I recommend parking, immediately crossing half the market, and sitting down in front of her, at which point you should order an egg al comal (a fried egg) and a memela con tasajo (a memela with grilled flank steak). Then you wait for your food, rubbing your hands in anticipation. La Güera doesn't stop moving. She tosses tortillas onto the comal, she stirs the coffee and the atole (a hot, thick masa-based drink), she grills the tasajo and makes the salsa in a molcajete. Before you know it, you find a tasty memela and steaming hot coffee in front of you. There's a feeling of family at the stand; everyone sings La Güera's praises, and she barely allows herself the luxury of a little laugh and a joke among the pots and smoke.

The rest of the Mercado de Abastos is more enjoyable after you've made your pilgrimage to La Güera, where in her eternal good faith and good mood she fills the bellies of buyers, vendors, distracted tourists, and those who come from far away to sell their products.

4. MOLOTES DEL MERCADO REFORMA

Mercado Hidalgo (known as the Mercado de la Colonia Reforma)
Palmeras s/n, Reforma, Oaxaca, Oaxaca

The Mercado de la Colonia Reforma—officially Mercado Hidalgo—is a neighborhood market: small, practical, and very bright. While it may not have the chaotic charm nor the astounding variety of the Mercado 20 de Noviembre or the Mercado de Abastos, there is a stand that has any competition beat: the one selling molotes, stuffed and fried corn dough or masa. I like to have a quick breakfast here when I am working at Café Casa Oaxaca, just a couple of blocks away. It's partly a practical decision, because it's on my way, but there is a deeper reason as well: these molotes remind me of the fairs of my childhood, of going to the plaza when there's a celebration, of strolling with my family. While all of Oaxaca's street food is comforting, molotes are perhaps our truest comfort food.

Molotes from Oaxaca's central valley differ greatly from what are called molotes on the Isthmus. Corn masa is delicately wrapped around a filling of potatoes and chorizo. This is deep-fried, resulting in an irresistible snack that is crunchy on the outside and soft on the inside. This simple, marvelous mixture is shaped by expert hands into the silhouette of a bullet, which is then delicately dropped into bubbling hot oil. The molote is lightly fried, then drained. After it has cooled a little, it is served in butcher paper that doubles as a plate on which the molote is dressed with crema, cheese, and red or green salsa. It's the only thing sold at this stand. The texture, temperature, flavor, and everything else are just as they should be.

5. LA TECA

Violetas 200 A, Reforma, Oaxaca, Oaxaca

Going to La Teca is like coming home, thanks to the presence of Deyanira Aquino, the proprietor and head chef. Deyanira is a born host with the warmth of a friend who welcomes you to her leafy patio with a mezcal and a smile. Her hospitality is frank, her personality is strong, and her feminine energy undeniable.

The Isthmus of Tehuantepec has mountains in the west, plains in the east, and the coast to the south. The entire region is in an area of warm tropical climate, except at certain elevations of the mountain range, where winds from the Pacific provide a comparatively cooler climate. People come to La Teca to try the typical flavors of the Isthmus, a variation of Oaxacan food that, due to its geography, offers sweet, coastal nuances. I come here with my friends when I want to clear my mind of work and reset my palate.

On a patio full of bougainvillea, trays of garnachas begin to emerge: little fried masa bowls with shredded meat, red chile salsa, and pickled onions and plantain molotes with crema and cheese—quite different from the little balls of masa from the central valley that bear the same name—together with agua fresca and beer. These snacks are reason enough for multiple return visits to La Teca. Then comes the estofado de boda, a fruity mole with a complex, enveloping flavor, accompanied by a purée of potatoes from the Isthmus, distinct for the way it incorporates chopped pickled vegetables. To finish there are corn tamalitos, small and fluffy tamals, served with crema and cheese. But the real dessert is Deyanira's smile and the warmth of mezcal in your throat.

6. EL MANGALITO

Cosijoeza 200, La Soledad, Villa de Zaachila, Oaxaca

In Villa de Zaachila, some six kilometers from the town where I was born, you'll find a family-run restaurant called El Mangalito. It's important to note that they only open two days a week, Wednesdays and Thursdays, which is the time it takes to butcher and eat two pigs.

El Mangalito is a patio with long, shared tables that are always full of people. At the back is an open-air kitchen. Musicians with an amplifier sing rancheras (a genre of traditional music dating back to pre-Revolution times) to recorded tracks from the roof of the kitchen. At a distance you can see the fogones, the comal, the butcher board, and a blue truck that makes the supply runs. From the tables you can see the roofing, above which pork skins hang from improvised implements, waiting to be made into chicharrón. This is a family business. Sitting at a table, the owner's grandmother stuffs pork filling into chiles rellenos to be battered and fried. The grandfather observes a cauldron bubbling with boiling oil. The biuses, pork offal such as tripe, kidney, and uterus that are deepfried in lard, are being prepared. The daughters wash, serve, slice, attend, and administer. The sons-in-law come in and out. The grandchildren get home from school and toss their backpacks in a corner so that they can help their parents with the work in the kitchen. When you order, you only have to say the number of people sitting at the table. The menu? Pork. Every part of the pig. The first dish is essentially a pork salad. A well-balanced assortment of rosy, pickled pork skin, along with onions and native allspice berries, golden crackling, juicy white meat, and pork back fat. The vinegary tartness nicely complements and cuts the unctuous fat. On the side are avocados, tomatoes, radishes, and lettuce. Then come the beans cooked with pig feet and the stuffed chiles de agua. Here, all who love pork eat until they burst. Every bite is lightly spicy, but a sip of mezcal immediately takes care of that. The mezcal left on the table in plastic water bottles can compete with the most exclusive mezcals served in the world's most elegant restaurants.

El Mangalito is a true regional favorite. There's nothing more to say. It's pure eating, pure enjoyment.

7. MERCADO DE TLACOLULA

Weekly market, Tercera Sección, Tlacolula de Matamoros, Oaxaca

You have to go to Tlacolula on Sunday, because that's the day for the tianguis, and not just any tianguis—it's one of the most important in Oaxaca and, perhaps, the world. Tianguis are special markets. On Sundays all the producers from surrounding towns come together to create an offering that is incomparable in quality, freshness, and variety. The prices are also very good, because you're buying directly from the producer. It's the closest thing to a pre-Hispanic tianguis to be found just a few miles from the capital of Oaxaca. The tianguis occupies the town's main street and side streets. The part of the market that happens under a roof is open all week, but it's only on Sundays that you find the most impressive array of products, and the most vitality. On sale are ingredients as well as instruments for cooking and agriculture.

I often go to shop at the tianguis, but above all, I go to eat. Visiting the Mercado de Tlacolula is a ritual in several parts. To begin with there are the famous local sweet pastries or pan dulce: the outstanding pan de yema, or yolk bread, lighter than air with a golden interior and a brown soft crust sprinkled with sesame seeds. Pan de cazuela, or crockpot bread, given that name because of the clay pot in which it was originally made. Because these often broke, pan de cazuela are now baked in repurposed sardine cans. Oaxacan spiced chocolate and raisins hide in its cinnamon-and-anise-infused dough. Along with pan de manteca (lard bread) and hojaldras, a simple pan dulce bejeweled by fuchsia-stained sugar, these typical regional items are always eaten with a cup of hot chocolate. Next comes the barbacoa enchilada, with its consommé, tacos, and salsas to dress them—and, of course, the mezcal.

After taking a spin around the market to make purchases and visit the church, it's time to go to the smoke-filled aisle. This activity has its own etiquette: first you select a carnicería or butcher shop to buy tasajo, cecina enchilada, and chorizo. At another stand you buy tortillas, avocados, grilled onions, radishes, and chiles de agua, which are the sides for the meats.

Then, back to the shopping. I already have a metate, a tablecloth, some lemons, some guajes. But I can't leave without trying a glass of tejate (a beverage made with corn and cacao). There's a stand so famous that you can't see the end of the line. I consider this the best tejate in the region.

GLOSSARY

Acitronar To put an onion or any other raw vegetable in hot oil and allow it to sauté, stirring constantly, until the vegetable softens and becomes brighter in color.

Anafre A small oven or grill in which to cook with fire, typically portable.

Asadura An animal's viscera. Primarily, the liver, lungs, and heart. They are usually eaten fried, grilled, or as part of a stew. This term is generally used in the plural.

Asiento Asiento means sediment. It is the used lard that results from making chicharrón, or fried pork skin, that may or may not have bits of chicharrón left over in the bottom. What is more commonly used now, but goes by the same name, is a mixture of virgin lard and asiento.

Atole Also known as atole blanco, atole de masa, or atole de maíz (white atole, dough atole, or corn atole), it is a hot thick drink made of corn that has been cooked and ground. The white atole can be drunk as is, or flavored with spices or fruit.

Barbacoa In Mexico this term is used for roasted lamb, beef, or goat prepared in a hole in the ground that is used as an oven; the surface of the oven remains open and the firewood that heats the meat is placed at the bottom. Ovens in the ground have their roots in Mayan culture, where fish was cooked outdoors.

Calabacita güichi Tatuma, an heirloom squash variety that's round, and has a mildly sweet flavor and firm texture that turns to buttery flesh when cooked.

Calabaza tamalayota This squash is extremely similar to what is known as pumpkin in the U.S. Its name comes from the Nahuatl word tamalayohtli, which means "squash tamal." It's a very large variety, with orange pulp and a thick rind with pronounced grooves. It is principally eaten candied, and its seeds, pepitas, are used to made pipián.

Camote A type of sweet potato that is yellow, purple, or white in color. It is used to prepare several kinds of traditional Mexican sweets, and has a floury texture, sweet taste, and high starch content. The word is derived from the Nahuatl camotli.

Chamoy A condiment made from a base of dried fruit, chile, salt, and sugar. Its flavor is at once sweet, spicy, and sour. It's generally found in powdered form, but is also sometimes seen as a liquid. Its origins lie outside of Mexico, but here it has taken root as a favorite condiment for fruit and potato chips, among other items.

Chapulín or Chapulines The Mexican term for grasshoppers. The ones sold in the central valley tend to be farmed in alfalfa fields. They are sold in different sizes, by spoonful or cupful. The smallest ones have the most delicate flavor and are a bit more expensive than the larger ones.

Chayote Edible plant belonging to the gourd family, also called vegetable pear or mirliton. One variety commonly found in Oaxaca is bright green and covered in spines.

Chepiche This herb is used to flavor many different dishes, though it's most often found in beans and tlayudas.

Chepil (*Crotalaria longirostrata*) A leafy vegetable often used as an herb that grows in the fields during the rainy season. It has a potent aroma and a flavor similar to verdolaga (purslane) or baby spinach. Some species of *Crotalaria* are toxic, so you must be careful not to confuse chepil with other similar plants while gathering. It's a good source of vegetable protein.

Chichilo This mole requires a very laborious and complicated preparation; in Oaxaca it's made for special occasions such as funerals. Its characteristic black color is obtained from the mix of black chile, chilcuacle negro, chile pasilla, chile mulato, and charred tortillas.

Chigol This member of the community serves mezcal during festivities and their preparations—the person who makes sure that everyone who arrives to help or to have breakfast or lunch drinks their mezcal little by little.

Chilate 1. A beverage similar to atole that is made with toasted corn masa and cacao; in Oaxaca the custom is to add chile, but there are variations with cinnamon, piloncillo, or ground rice. 2. A stew made with beef or chicken that may contain chile guajillo, onion, and herbs. The Oaxacan version uses chile costeño and tomato with some kind of meat as the main ingredients.

Chile ancho This chile has a ruddy color and a rough texture. Its brick-red color is often used to tint stews. It is one of the most commonly used chiles in Mexican cooking.

Chile chilhuacle Its name comes from the Nahuatl chilhuactli, meaning "old chile." There are three varieties of chilhuacle: black, red, and yellow. Each colors a different kind of mole. Its flavor is moderately spicy.

Chile chiltepín This name refers to a wide variety of small chiles of Mexican origin, all very spicy. They measure around ½ to ¾ inch and are a green color when not yet ripe, bright red as they mature, and brownish red when they dry.

Chile de agua When young, this chile has a light green color; as it matures it becomes orange. It's rarely used dried, and it's quite spicy. It's a challenge to find it outside Oaxaca, where it's widely used. It's largely known for its presence in mole amarillo and in chichilo negro, although it's also used to make spicy salsas.

Chile guajillo Dried chile with a reddish color and smooth, shiny skin. Often used to give color and consistency to guisos, moles, and salsas. When fresh it's known as the chile mirasol. This is one of the easiest chiles to find in Mexico.

Chile meco This is the name for a chile jalapeño that has been dried but not smoked. It's a light brown color and very spicy. When smoked it is known as a chile chipotle, except in Veracruz, where it's called chile seco.

Chile morita A dried, smoked chile; smaller than the chile mora, but similar. It gets its name from its purple skin. This chile is very spicy but also has a certain sweetness.

Chile mulato This is a dried chile, blackish brown in color, meaty and with a thick skin. Its shape and color are similar to the chile ancho, but it has a different flavor, as the mulato is sweet and rarely spicy. It's important in the preparation of dark moles, such as mole poblano.

Chile pasilla A dried chile with a blackish brown color. Its taste is moderately spicy, and it's used to make salsas like salsa borracha, as well as moles, adobos, and a dish called el revoltijo. When fresh, this chile is known as chile chilaca.

Chile pasilla oaxaqueño (or mixe) A smoked, dried chile with shiny red skin and a triangular shape. Its spiciness varies—sometimes it can be sweet like chile morita, sometimes it's very spicy. It's hard to find outside Oaxaca.

Chile serrano Also known as chile verde, this variety is native to Mexico and frequently consumed here and is characterized by its small size and cylindrical shape sometimes ending in a point. It's considered spicy and is generally prepared with its seeds and veins, which are also spicy, intact.

Chilmolera or chilmolero 1. A person dedicated to making mole. 2. An instrument similar to a molcajete, but made of clay, in which the chiles are ground to make mole or other salsas.

Chochoyote Also known as chochoyota, chochoyo, or chochoyón, these little balls of corn masa (the same masa used in tortillas) are used in many traditional Mexican dishes. They are small dumplings distinguished by the depression in their center made by the fingers that shape them.

Comal or comales A circular cooking surface that can be made of clay or metal. They are usually placed directly over flame, whether on a stovetop or a fogón, or even atop the embers of a fire. They are most commonly used in making tortillas; however, they have other uses including toasting, roasting, or charring ingredients.

Epazote An aromatic plant native to Latin America. It is distinguished by its particular scent and pronounced flavor. As a herb, it is used often in Mexican cooking. It is indispensable for making frijoles de la olla, caldo tlalpeño, and mole verde.

Flor de calabaza As its name ("flower of squash") implies, this is the flower produced by the calabaza (squash) plant. Its petals are yellow and orange in color. The species most used for culinary purposes is the *Curcubita pepo.*

Fogón The place in the kitchen that contains the fire where food is cooked. It may be an open fire or even a metal apparatus, fed by wood, gas, or electricity. In indigenous regions of Mexico this is the most special place in the kitchen, as it serves both as a hub of warmth and a cooking station.

Frijolón Also known as ayocote, from the Nahuatl ayecohtli. The largest type of bean in Mexico, measuring close to 1 inch. Their color varies from purple to black, gray, brown, red, amber, tan, and marbled. The plant produces edible red flowers in February.

Garnachas The term garnacha can encompass a wide array of food items that are usually made with corn dough, cooked on a comal or fried in lard or vegetable oil. It can be filled with an assortment of things, as well as topped with sour cream, cheese, lettuce, and salsa. Gorditas, sopes, huaraches, molotes, flautas, tlacoyos, or even quesadillas all fall into the garnacha category. These snacks, or antojitos (small cravings), are traditional, local, even regional fast foods that are commonly sold by street vendors.

Guacachile Don't be fooled by the name: although it sounds like guacamole, it's really just chiles. The green tone of guacachile comes from chiles serranos; there are no avocados in the recipe. The procedure for making guacachile is closer to that for making mayonnaise, and as with that condiment, you must keep it from separating.

Guajes 1. A squash with a wide base that, once dried, is used to store and carry liquids and other products. 2. A very large variety of acacia tree that grows in warm regions and produces a large bean containing edible seeds. 3. A type of tomato.

Guajolote A bird native to Mexico similar to a turkey, highly appreciated for its meat, characterized by its featherless head and neck and fleshy red membrane, which loosely hangs under it.

Guías de calabaza Squash plant runners (guides). The tender part of the plant is used to make soup along with the squash and its flowers.

Guiso Stew.

Hierba de Conejo Wild herb or quelite, found in the central valley of Oaxaca during the rainy season. It's used in various stews and imparts an earthy, slightly anise-like aroma.

Hoja de aguacate This is the leaf of the avocado plant. Depending on the recipe it can be used either fresh or dried, roasted or cooked. In Oaxaca it is ground for use in moles, chichilos, and several other regional dishes. Be warned, some avocado leaves are toxic.

Hojaldra Myriad of pastries, sweet or savory, that take different forms depending on where in Mexico you are. In Oaxaca it is a simple pan dulce bejeweled with fuchsia-stained sugar.

Hoja santa Also known as hierba santa or acuyo. This herb is utilized as a condiment for its anise flavor, and is very common in Oaxacan cooking.

Huacal, huacales An open crate of wooden slats used mainly to transport fruits and vegetables.

Huitlacoche An edible fungus that lives as a parasite on the cobs of the corn plant; it appears as a grayish outbreak inside the kernels on the cob, and when it matures it acquires a black color. It is a highly coveted delicacy in Mexico and often prepared as a guiso served with tortillas or other snacks.

Jicapextle From the Nahuatl xicalli, which means jícara (see next entry), and petztli, meaning "something polished." On the Isthmus of Tehuantepec this is the name for a jícara of any size painted with floral designs. It is used to hold fruit, tortillas, and other items.

Jícara A small bowl, typically made from the fruit of the calabash tree (*Crescentia alata*). The gourd is cut in half, hollowed, and left to dry, resulting in two half-sphered jícaras. These can then be carved, painted, or used as is to serve food or beverages. It is commonly found in rural indigenous communities in southern Mexico.

Jilotear A verb describing the moment when the flowers, or jilotes, begin to sprout, followed by the young corn cobs. In the milpa, it refers to when the corn begins to appear on the plants.

Macerar To macerate, i.e., the process of giving flavor to or preserving raw food, which consists of leaving the food soaking for a determined time, be it in liquor, oil, vinegar, lime juice, or another liquid. The food is impregnated with the flavor and absorbs part of the liquid in which it is soaked.

Martajar To grind/pound in a molcajete but not to the point of forming a paste or pulverizing; you are looking to keep chunks or larger pieces of what you're grinding/crushing.

Masa harina This corn flour, usually powdered, is used to make tortillas, tamales, and other dishes that call for nixtamalized corn. Maseca is an example of a brand-name masa harina.

Mayordomía A celebration in which a banquet, music, and mezcal are offered to loved ones. Mayordomías may be thrown for important occasions such as a wedding or a saint's feast, or they may happen for no particular reason.

Mayordomo To be the mayordomo, the captain of the celebration, is to take on the responsibility of sponsoring and organizing the mayordomía for fellow community members.

Memela This name comes from tlaxcalmimilli, a combination of the Nahuatl words tlaxcalli, which means "tortilla," and mimilli, which means "long." As opposed to a regular tortilla, a memela is thick and its borders form a little rim so that it can hold a filling.

Metate From the Nahuatl metlatl, meaning "stone made of hands." A long flat stone upon which another cylindrical stone is used to grind ingredients, mainly corn. It is designed to be used sitting on the floor.

Metlapil No longer commonly used, in some places this term still refers to the pestle, or mano, of a metate. It is made from the same stone as the metate.

Milpa Literally, "planted lot." A parcel of land planted with several crops chosen to take advantage of the characteristics of each. It mainly refers to a field planted with corn and associated crops: beans, squash, fava beans, tomatoes, miltomates, etc.

Miltomate This is a variety of green tomato, small in size, that is grown at milpas. It is similar to a tomatillo, which can be substituted, and comes covered with a thick shell of leaves that are easily removed. In Oaxacan heirloom varieties its coloration ranges from green to purple.

Molcajete A mortar made of volcanic stone that is used to crush different ingredients, from tomatoes to nuts.

Molcajetear The act and effect of grinding something in a molcajete.

Molinillo A kitchen utensil used, among other things, to mix and aerate hot chocolate. It is composed of two pieces, a cylindrical stick and a thick wheel at the lower end that spins from side to side in order to beat the liquid in which it is submerged. The traditional Mexican molinillo is carved from one piece of wood.

Molotes Stuffed and deep-fried corn dough or masa.

Nahuatl Living Aztec language. When referring to the language the word means "pleasant clear tongue."

Nixtamal The process by which corn kernels are soaked in a water and lime (calcium hydroxide) solution before they can be ground and made into masa for tortillas.

Pan amarillito A traditional Oaxacan sweet bread that is prepared with whole wheat flour and may, on occasion, contain anise.

Panela or piloncillo A sweetener made from raw cane sugar syrup that is cooked, whipped, then cast in a mold. Piloncillo is conic in shape, while panela is square.

Pan mollete Similar to pan amarillito, this is a bread made with wheat flour and a mix of piloncillo, anise, and sesame seeds.

Piojito An aromatic herb that is used in the central valley of Oaxaca to give flavor to soups; it is present in the famous sopa de guías and is often used as a substitute for chepil. It can be found fresh or dried at markets.

Piquete When a drink has a shot of liquor added to it, usually rum or aguardiente, it's said to come con piquete, or "with a sting."

Pitiona A shrub from the verbena family. Tall and aromatic, with velvety leaves. It is a well-known condiment in Oaxaca as it is one of the main herbs used in mole amarillo. It has medicinal properties and can be used to aid digestion.

Quelites From the Nahuatl quilitl (vegetable). The name refers to certain edible leaves or herbs frequently used in Mexican cooking. There are many varieties. Usually quelites are boiled and seasoned with garlic.

Quesillo Also known in the rest of Mexico as queso oaxaca, Oaxacan cheese, or Oaxacan string cheese. This fresh white cheese is made with cow's milk and has a mellow flavor. It is characterized by the long strips into which it's stretched once the milk solidifies, which are then rolled up to make little balls that look like skeins of yarn.

Queso istmeño As its name, "cheese of the Isthmus," implies, this is a cheese from the Isthmus of Tehuantepec. A very dry cheese, similar to Parmesan. It is usually served grated or crumbled over a finished dish.

Rollo de hierbas de olor A mix of aromatic herbs, which may include thyme, marjoram, oregano, and rosemary, fresh or dried.

Segueza A souplike stew made from a base of chile chilcostle or guajillo with tomatoes. It is thickened with dried corn, toasted, and broken up on the metate, and is very traditional in the central valley of Oaxaca.

Sopa de chepiles Soup made with squash, squash flowers, and chepil, and thickened with masa (corn dough).

Tamales or tomal Masa or corn dough stuffed with meat, chicken, beans, or other ingredients, wrapped in corn or banana leaves, and steamed.

Tapesco From the Nahuatl tlapechtli, which means framework or grid of branches or boards. A man-made grill where food is dried, cooked, or smoked.

Tejate From the Nahuatl textli (masa) and atl (water). This is a foamy beverage of pre-Hispanic origin. Made from a corn and cacao base, it is traditionally served in jícaras for mid-morning refreshment.

Tejolote A pestle. A stone utensil, also known as the mano, used to crush items in a molcajete.

Teocintle The antecedent of what is now known as maíz, corn, from which corn was cultivated by the ancient inhabitants of Mesoamerica.

Tetela A food similar to a memela, but with a triangular shape and bean filling. This shape is not found elsewhere in Mexico, only in Oaxaca and Puebla.

Tianguis From the Nahuatl tianquiztli (market) and tiamiqui (to sell, to market), this is a market that occurs in a plaza or on the street. Products sold range from clothing to ready-to-eat food to fresh produce.

Tichinda A variety of clam with a greenish black shell that is white inside. Its natural habitat is in the waters of the Pacific mangroves, which is why it's found in many dishes from the Oaxacan coast, from soups to tamales.

Tlacoyo A dish made with a thick corn masa tortilla. Although its shape may vary, a tlacoyo is filled with pastes made from beans, alverjón (a relative of the chickpea), chicharrón, or fava bean. After cooking it on the comal, it is dressed with salsa, cilantro, and onion.

Tlayuda A large (about 12-inch), round, thin corn tortilla. A raw flat disk of dough is placed on a comal, and once it's cooked through, it's set next to the embers until it becomes leathery and brittle. In Oaxaca it is often reheated with pork fat, refried beans, and an assortment of ingredients such as flank steak, sausage, cheese, and salsa.

Tomate guajillo Guajillo tomatoes, sometimes called saladettes, are the most common tomatoes anywhere in Mexico. Roma tomatoes are a good substitute.

Tomate rastrojo, cuatomate, tomate milpa The cuatomate is a plant that belongs to the nightshade family of vegetables. It produces a type of tomato that's small and round, and grows in clusters. Its color may vary from white to green, or orange and red. It is similar to a cherry tomato, but more acidic. Originally a wild species, in other parts of the country it's also called tinguaraque.

Tomate riñón An heirloom tomato found in Oaxaca. It's similar to a Marmande, or something between Bull's Heart and beefsteak. It's meaty, sweet, and extremely fragile, which is why it does not travel well.

Tortilla A flat disk of cooked corn masa or wheat flour; it may be made by hand or machine. Tortillas are one of the foundations of Mexican food, and their size varies from region to region and according to the dish in which they are to be used. They accompany almost any food and form the base for tacos, enchiladas, totopos, chilaquiles, and tostadas.

Tostadas Corn tortillas toasted or fried until they harden and acquire a crunchy texture.

Totomoztle or totomoxtle The leaves that cover cobs of corn. When dried they are used to wrap and cook tamales.

Totopos Totopo is a tortilla chip. Totopos in the Isthmus of Tehuantepec are different; they are round, flat, and dotted with holes. They're cooked in a comixcal, a clay pot with hollow bottom that is encircled by adobe blocks and sand, and sealed with mud. Wood is burned at the bottom of the pot, and when the embers are ready, the totopo is attached (with the moisture of the dough) to the inner wall of the pot and baked there until it hardens.

Vela The most important celebrations of the Isthmus of Tehuantepec, considered one of the most deeply rooted traditions in Oaxaca. These events honor the patron saints of families, groups, trades, or places. The celebration coincides with the start of the corn-growing period and the beginning of the rainy season.

Verdolaga A leafy vegetable from India, purslane in English. Its flavor is tart, but its soft texture makes it a delicious vegetable for salads and many guisos. Highly appreciated in Mexico, they are typically prepared in a stew with pork.

Xoconostle The fruit of a type of prickly pear cactus, only used to make sweets in syrup or coated in sugar.

ACKNOWLEDGMENTS

Kitchen credits: Cooks from La Raya de Zimatlán: Teresa Olmedo, Raquel Olmedo, Rosalina Olmedo, Áurea Olmedo, Clemencia Olmedo, Mercedes Lavariega, and Zenaida López. Cooks at Hotel Casa Oaxaca / Restaurante Casa Oaxaca / Guzina Oaxaca: Rafael Villalobos, Norma Velazco, María Velazco, Israel Sosa, Odilón García, Carlos Galán and Enid Vélez Raga. Recipe Testers: Carla Altesor, Juana García, Arturo Villaseñor, Gabriela Mota, Andrea Cazares, Daniel Carrillo, Michelle Puente, Meyer Feriarte, David Estrada, Takashi Miyamoto, Cristina Pérez, José Ignacio Chapela, Marta Reyes Retana, Mirena Rivas, Keña Marcos, Demián Barba, Genoveva Bautista, Sara Santiago, María Álvarez, and Luisa Reyes Retana.

Text credits: María Álvarez, Carla Altesor, Carmen Castillo, and Luisa Reyes Retana.

This book was made possible thanks to the generosity of Juan Garay.

Thanks to Liliana Mexueiro, Marco Ruiz, Jesús Ruiz, Norma Ruiz, Lourdes Ruiz, Iván Saldaña, Emilio Chapela, Santiago Ruiseñor, Roberto Velázquez, Isabel Ferreira, Rodolfo Ogarrio, Ana Ogarrio, Soledad Díaz, Alexandra Haas and Zakarías Zafra, Diego Cruz, Diego Cruz Jr., Sergio Ruiz, Rafael Olmedo, Isabel Meneses, Joaquin Ruiz, Bernabé Martínez, Armando Castellanos, Daniel Castellanos, Blair Richardson, Jessica Sandoval, Sonia Mozden, and Odilón Reyes.

At Knopf, thank you to Kelly Blair, Kevin Bourke, Sara Eagle, Anna Knighton, Lisa Montebello, Sarah New, and Tom Pold.

Thanks to Lacey Pipkin for translating the book into English.

We made this book with the following people in mind: Alíah, Lara, Alejandro, Paulo, Isabela, Emilia, Julián, Sabino, Ana, and Andrés.

INDEX

Page numbers in *italics* refer to illustrations.

A NOTE ON THE TYPE

The text of this book was set in Calluna, a typeface designed by Jos Buivenga (b. 1965) and released in 2009. Calluna has refreshing characteristics that individualize the font, such as the slope of the serifs on the descenders of the p and q. Its italic variant takes on a more flowing, calligraphic feel.

Composed by North Market Street Graphics, Lancaster, Pennsylvania
Printed and bound by C&C Offset, China
Designed by Anna B. Knighton